MATRIX MAN

How To Become Enlightened, Happy & Free In An Illusion World

MATRIX MAN

How To Become Enlightened, Happy & Free In An Illusion World

S. F. Howe

Diamond Star Press
Los Angeles

MATRIX MAN: How To Become Enlightened, Happy & Free In An Illusion World

Trade Paperback
ISBN13: 9780977433551
ISBN 10: 0977433552

Published by Diamond Star Press

For finders of truth,

far and wide

FREE GIFT

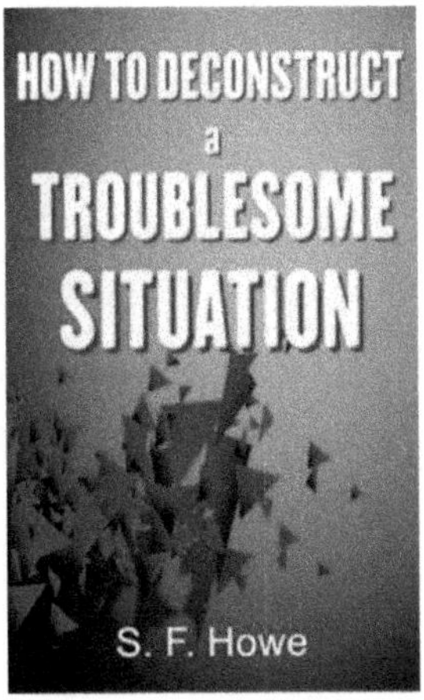

As my thanks to you for reading ***Matrix Man: How To Become Enlightened, Happy & Free In An Illusion World,*** I would like you to have the free bonus report, "How to Deconstruct a Troublesome Situation." This bonus gift is an important addition to the material in this book and will help you implement its teachings.

If you apply the technique in this report, you will not only discover the many ways in which your mental and emotional conditioning interferes with your peaceful inner state but you will also learn how to clear and detach from the negative emotional reactions that upset your day. To get your free gift, just go to http://bit.ly/DeconstructSituation.

BOOKS BY S. F. HOWE

Matrix Man
How To Become Enlightened, Happy And Free In An Illusion World

The Top Ten Myths Of Enlightenment
Exposing The Truth About Spiritual Enlightenment That Will Set You Free!

The Bringer
Waking Up To The Mind Control Programs Of The Matrix Reality

Secrets Of The Plant Whisperer
How To Care For, Connect, And Communicate With Your House Plants

Your Plant Speaks!
How To Use Your Houseplant As A Therapist
Coming Soon!

Vision Board Success
How To Get Everything You Want With Vision Boards!

Sex Yoga
The 7 Easy Steps To A Mind-Blowing Kundalini Awakening!

Transgender America
Spirit, Identity, And The Emergence Of The Third Gender

Morning Routine For Night Owls
How To Supercharge Your Day With A Gentle Yet Powerful Morning Routine!

When Nothing Else Works
How To Cure Your Lower Back Pain Fast!

TABLE OF CONTENTS

AUTHOR PREFACE

This book is targeted toward advanced truth seekers. It is also recommended for new age and new thought spiritual pathers who are hungry for something more.

For all who enter here—you need not take off your shoes, but you are kindly asked to leave your 'sacred cows' at the door.

Introduction

THE SECRET OF CREATION

I have been accessing information from my higher self since my spiritual awakening a long time ago. As a result, I wrote thousands of pages of spiritual philosophy about the nature of reality, but never felt called to reveal that work to the public.

Finally, after considerable nudging by my higher self, I have allowed this book to be published for the modern audience. This introductory chapter contains excerpts from a more than thirty page preliminary discourse that I received from my higher dimensional self prior to writing this manuscript. I have selected for you the sections that I believe will best prepare you for the material that follows.

We are your guides and guardians, your teachers and friends. Yet we are also you, parts of you with access to the higher dimensional knowledge you long for, the truth and wisdom your heart craves like your body craves physical nourishment. This teaching begins the path of knowledge that opens into many byways and highways, bringing you to heights of understanding and awareness of the secrets of creation, the truth about physical reality, and the mastery over all that appears within and without you. This is what you seek and what you shall teach. It is what you shall live and demonstrate and in that way, your teachings will be the authentic truth of your soul.

Be not afraid of the truth or of the knowledge that resides within you awaiting your reception. The path opens before you now, as it has for many years in the illusion of time. The time is always now, the now is always here. Thus, you can begin without fear, without a sense of guilt or loss. You are whole now and this information is awaiting you, serving the highest purpose we can conceive of for a human lifetime – to bring into your awareness while in the 'story,' the truth of reality. With acceptance of truth comes power and healing. The means of healing becomes obvious when the truth is known and accepted. The restoration of power is automatic when the truth is realized.

Your power awaits, your healing awaits, as does your ability to heal and empower others. Do not delay any further. The now is here. Your time has come. Accept the mantel of grace which is being bestowed upon you, and with the purity of a soul that has been scorched in the fires of life until alchemically restored to essence, receive what we provide. You will be grateful for grasping the scepter, most especially when you see what is being given and the power, meaning and beauty of the work.

Truth is the healer. The highest truth has never been told. Be brave, dear one, and let us tell the truth through you and allow the power of love to burst through the avenue of truth you create to heal a world contracted by lies and hate. Love is the healer, but love cannot enter where truth has not opened the way. Be the wayshower, Beloved, the opener, and trust that your words will reach those who can hear, who most need them, and that you will be safe, surrounded as if in a cradle of cotton, such is the love that guides and protects you.

The truth is radical, dear one. So radical, most will not accept it, most cannot face it. But enough seek to know, that you will have your work cut out for you. You are one of the few willing to face the truth, yet even you have delayed this work.

The secret is that you create reality, literally. You do not seek, you create. The teaching, seek and you shall find, always puts the desire outside of your grasp. It is a recipe for failure.

You create what you desire, as if molding it out of clay. That is the powerful way to live because it is the way of truth. And the proof of truth is in the results. A teaching that cannot be proven by results is not in alignment with the truth. A teaching that puts your power out of your hands is not a teaching of the truth. A teaching that has you believing power must be reclaimed is toying with you.

There is no separation between your greater self and the self in the story. The greater self does not torment the self in the story for purposes of learning or testing or idle curiosity. The greater self carries the gauntlet for the story self until the self in the story picks up the gauntlet of its own accord. The only thing that ever happens is a subtle shift in consciousness wherein the self in the story recognizes itself to be the greater self.

When the self in the story recognizes itself as the greater self in the widest sense possible, the sense of absolute truth, the self consciously creates anything it wishes. There are no predetermined endings to the story once the self picks up the gauntlet. The predetermination is a default program that can be overridden if self awakens to its true identity. Identity is the only issue at stake. Who are you? What are you? Once the identity code is cracked, the self in the story receives a full download of power.

The game is simple – can you wake up in the story in the same sense as you may wake up inside a dream and realize you're dreaming. The lucid dream and the lucid life are one and the same – a realization of the absolutely dream-like nature of reality and your ability to alter it by the simple act of recognizing you are in a dream. But just telling yourself it is a dream is not the answer. The true awareness of the dream can only be proven by one's ability to alter the dream. Or you may choose to continue in the dream as is, aware of your creative ability but not choosing to exercise it in that moment. Reality is an absolutely fluid state and has no solidity whatsoever. Thus, that which we call reality is in truth not real.

We use the term, 'the work,' to refer to the great task you chose and agreed to of bringing forth the highest truth about the nature of reality that has been accessed in your world to date. This truth is to some extent geared to the times within which you find yourself. It has been geared to assist your readers in ways that are relevant and meaningful to them here and now. In receiving this information, your readers activate the transformational power of truth, and their lives will never be the same.

Now, on to the work.

Chapter 1

THE NATURE OF REALITY

There are some realizations that can only be understood once they are attained. They are not likely to be attained without prior consideration of certain ideas and an experimental approach to everyday reality. This playing with ideas and reality sets the stage for new understandings to take shape and eventually a shift in consciousness that permits continual realization of the actual state of reality.

In the actual state of reality, you are creating your experience moment by moment. It does not pre-exist. There is no world so to speak, no history, no future. The teachings of science that, for example, date the fossils and carbon layers of a planet are illusions that help convince the default player (the story-you) that the world is real and pre-exists. A default player may live their entire life without ever allowing themself to question this 'real world.' The player may believe themself to be attaining spiritual knowledge and awareness, but has never really cracked the code of consciousness.

Those who are called to the truth desire to understand the nature of reality while inside the reality. They are the ones who seek to become lucid in the dream, in this case, the dream of reality. They understand that there is the dream of sleep and the dream of reality. Both are dreams, taking place in different aspects or 'dimensions' of consciousness.

If consciousness is viewed as a prism, it has innumerable facets, each facet a new dream of reality. There are as many realities as there are facets, and the facets are infinite because consciousness is infinite.

Reality is a fluid facet of consciousness for which there are infinite versions. However, each reality contains a default nature for the default player. The reality expands in potential as the consciousness of the player expands. These realities may be viewed as default software programs that are not customizable until you realize they can be customized.

Customization of a software reality depends on an awakening to the software's unreality and, therefore, to its potential for customization. Your existence is a mind game, games within games, yet with one connecting thread. The mind game ends when the player fully grasps his identity within the illusion and activates his power to create.

The ability of reality to appear real and solid is a characteristic of a software reality. It allows default players to follow a storyline without needing to penetrate the nature of reality. Many players do not wish to play with full awareness. It is a choice of the greater self before beginning the virtual reality story. Some greater selves have designed the story so that a default player does begin to desire fuller awareness and may be allowed to realize some of the truth that is available.

Each story allows for a different level of consciousness for the identity within the story. In this way greater selves run numerous stories simultaneously and experience the widest range of experiences. These stories cross time and space and appear to take place in the illusion past, present and future. Some may appear to take place on this planet, others in other locales. Some may appear to be human existences, elsewhere the player may express in other forms. The infinite potential for variety of story, identity, form and place makes for the widest possible engagement of a greater self as it explores its own consciousness.

All exploration of consciousness is occurring within the one living consciousness of the All That Is. The All

That Is is an eternal, immortal state of potentiality that has no other purpose than to explore its own potential. It has created an elaborate and ever-expanding creation with infinite facets in order to endlessly explore and expand its own awareness of being. As you awaken to your awareness of being the All That Is, you expand the All That Is into your story and awaken potentials that could not have previously manifested.

There is really only one game among the many – the game of awakening to being the All within the story. This awakening, when fully embraced, removes the dross of personality and replaces it with the freedom of impersonality. The result is an embodied identity with an unconditioned consciousness. When an identity is restored to unconditioned consciousness, they express the miraculous.

In the next chapter we will explore reality creation as it intimately relates to your Life-time.

Chapter 2

WHAT IS REAL?

It is in the interpreting of what-is that every moment of your life is judged, found guilty and sentenced. You feel imprisoned in one way or another throughout your life because you have sentenced yourself to prison.

Now, is it true that your greater self chose these events, or are you the chooser, you the dreamer in the story? Here it becomes important to remember the basics—there is only one you.

There is the you in the story and the greater you observing the story. Both are one and the same except that the you in the story operates through a filter that limits awareness and the ability to create.

Therefore, it is true that events—the raw facts of your everyday life and the conditions of that life—are created by the greater you observing the story. Is that you creating it moment by moment or is it running on autopilot? For example, is it a story that is being designed in the moment, much as an improvisational puppet show, or is there a preexisting script that is being acted out?

The answer is that the greater you, which is running numerous identities simultaneously in numerous stories in numerous 'worlds,' has sufficient consciousness in its unlimited self to be aware of being you at all moments in time. The story is both pre-scripted in broad outline and designed moment by moment.

The broad outline represents the default program. The moment by moment design represents customization of the program. The program can be customized by the greater self, but if the story self recognizes its true identity as the greater self, it can become aware of this customization while in the story and have the experience of customizing or creating its own reality.

At no time, however, does a story self who awakens to its greater self suddenly run off with the story in whatever direction it chooses. There is a very fine distinction being made here. The story self awakens to the greater self while in the story and has the subjective experience of creating its own reality. That creation is always the creation of the greater self and can never be the creation of a story self 'gone wild.'

Let us repeat that if a story self awakens to its greater identity while in the story, it simply becomes aware of the creative intent of that identity and creates as that identity, which is its true self. There are never two creations when it comes to events. However, there are two creations when it comes to the event created by the greater self and the interpretation created by the story self.

Enlightenment is the releasing of interpretation or judgment of the story by the story self along with its Self-realization of being the creator of the story.

There is only one consciousness. It is the great consciousness of the Living God, our own highest self, the absolute power behind all creation. That consciousness has subdivided itself infinitely, or expanded itself infinitely, however you wish to view it, in order to create an infinite exploration of its own ever-expanding potential.

Nothing is ruled out in this exploration, and nothing is real or solid. All that exists is being dreamed from within the Living God. All that exists lives inside the consciousness of that Living God. As such, all that exists is non-physical, even when presenting as an elaborate illusion of being physical.

Consciousness is not physical. Therefore, there is no such thing as a physical world. All realities are spiritual creations; all life forms are spiritual creations. God does not create physical worlds and physical people, just the illusion of a physical world and a physical person.

If you are not in a physical world and are not a physical person, then what are you? You are a Dream of God, who is your own true higher self.

Your Life-Time

What does that mean about your everyday life in this physical illusion? This physical illusion is no more real or substantial than your dreams at night. However, it is designed to have a certain illusion of solidity and continuity so that a specific story can be enacted in what is called your Life-Time.

Your Life-Time refers to a specific length of time in which your greater self runs a certain story. It is similar to a play or movie. It has a beginning, a middle and an end. You may view your Life-Time as, for example, a ninety year story with a specific setting, characters and events. You, the lead character, are given certain strengths and weaknesses, and the impetus to experience certain things in your Life-Time, known as your dreams or desires.

All of this is given at the start. The end is certain and is always known by the greater self. This is not a suspense thriller, intended to keep the greater self glued to its chair. It is a focused exploration of consciousness within a certain range of parameters.

Every existence has this constellation of properties and, for this reason, has meaning to the greater self. It would not have created that character and that existence if it did not desire to explore that specific aspect of itself.

From the point of view of the individual, there is only one story happening—their story—within the backdrop of a planet, a world of billions of other individuals. But one of the most interesting facets of creation is that none of this backdrop actually exists. It is created for the individual as they march the path of their Life-Time, by the greater self of the individual in order to provide atmosphere, stimulation and veracity for the Life-Time experience, much as sets, music and sound effects create the convincing illusion of reality in a movie.

From the point of view of the awakened individual, there is no pre-existing planet, no planetary history, and no concordant or pre-existing people in seemingly faraway lands. The details of history are set design, much as a period film relies on the costumes, objects, and dwellings of an era to recreate the period.

What does this mean for you today, right here, right now? It means that you have been launched by your own self into an illusion Life-Time experience for your own unique reasons and purposes. These reasons and purposes are known through the desires of your heart that whisper to you in quiet hours.

You have two choices. One is to experience your life as if it were real, taking seriously and literally the outer conditions that present themselves and morph around you. In this scenario you will believe your thoughts or interpretations of the events in your life and you will trust your emotional responses as truth. You will be subject to your outer reality and pushed this way and that as if by a fierce wind. Your emotions will rule your life. You will need to feel right all of the time and will do anything to defend your position. You will fear death and live by the law of survival of the fittest. You will attempt to strengthen yourself according to the methods espoused by your culture and media. You will constantly compare yourself to others to see how you stack up. You will subtly compete at all times with everyone to determine who is superior. The only reason you do this is to guarantee your own survival, as you live in fear of death at every moment in time. With death as the great slayer always at the back of your mind, you will contract your body and narrow your vision. You will try to stay safe and do what is recommended by the experts of your culture. You will be unconscious of who you really are, as that is the primary abdication of truth necessary for this kind of life to be lived. Yet it is the life of the vast majority.

The other choice is to recognize you are a story character invented by your greater self. You have a reason for being encapsulated within the desires and dreams of your heart. You are walking the path of your Life-Time, with nothing ahead of you until you place your foot down moment by moment and create the illusion of solid ground. Nothing is real, no one exists. It is all a play of consciousness, a literal illusion. You accept the stark events that occur as creations of your greater self. You understand that your emotional responses to these events do not define the truth about these events. In this way, you detach from your own emotions. You trust that living without interpretation, without judgment, is not only safe, it is hygienic, resulting in a clean, simple and uncomplicated moment by moment experience. You feel safe resting in unknowing, for within the need to know lies the seeds of all false teachings. You will never know what anything means or what anything is. You have the right and the freedom to decide for yourself what meaning or explanation you will attribute to That Which Is, if any. Yet your peace rests in allowing what-is to simply be without need for definition or interpretation.

Chapter 3

HOW REALITY IS CREATED

How is the reality within which you find yourself created? To simplify, every element that is potential in your world is encoded with a vibrational frequency, the DNA of creation. All potential objects are pre-created and pre-encoded, or are created and encoded as the story progresses, and then inserted into the story.

There is a default reality that is available for your consciousness the moment the story begins. It is not unlike hooking up to a virtual reality software program. When you put on your headset and flip the program switch, the story begins and you the observer and controller experience yourself as being within the story in a specific form with a specific identity. We will refer to the 'you' within the virtual software story as the story-you, the story self or the story identity. Sometimes we will use the terms 'the character within the story,' the persona, the extension, the avatar, the player or the default player. The 'you' observing the story is the infinite you or the greater self, although we might also reference your true self or Godself.

Here is an important point about the infinite you: it is not only the observer of the story, it is the creator of the story down to the tiniest detail, and it is the very substance of the story. In other words, the story plays out within the consciousness of the infinite you. There is nowhere in your story that the infinite you is not. It is both you, the character in the story, and everyone and everything around you. It is everywhere present.

The story is like a dream being enacted within the heart of consciousness, your consciousness. It is time-limited and time-defined, for certain events are pre-ordained. These include the moment and details of your birth, the moment and details of your death, and the many key events that occur in the time line of your Life-Time.

Each Life-Time has a time line, a virtual track that it follows like a train rides the railroad tracks. These tracks may at times involve switching to other tracks, returning over tracks, or going off the tracks, just as a train potentially does. Going off the tracks never occurs unless it has a key purpose in your destiny.

By destiny, we refer here to the intended purpose and function of your Life-Time. Yes, your life has meaning, but only for the greater self. If you understand that the greater self explores its own consciousness through you, then you will realize that the greater you has its own intents and purposes for running this Life-Time. It is on an experience-seeking mission to add to the total store of experience contained within itself, as well as a mental vacation of sorts from the lifestyle of an infinite being.

One might say that pleasure for an infinite being includes submitting itself to the illusion of being encapsulated in a physical body in a physical world and subjected to the rigors of that illusion while pursuing specific experiences within that illusion in order to gain experiential knowledge.

Your job as the story-you is to simply follow the track. The track is apparent if you are aware of the nature of reality. It is only a mass of confusion when you think you decide your life or you believe you can change track at will. If you ever thought you changed track through your will, it was an illusion, an interpretation of what really occurred. What really occurred was that your greater self moved tracks in order to pursue its intents and purposes as determined before the story began. This must bring you to conclude one thing only, which is that your greater self has always run your train and created the track.

Nothing in your life ever happened without the greater self creating it for you. Nothing in your life can ever happen without your greater self creating it for you. If something you wanted did not happen, it is because your greater self did not create it for you. It simply was not sufficiently important to the greater self or in alignment with the intents and purposes of the greater self.

Is This Your Intent and Purpose?

The smart story-you makes it their business to find out what are the intents and purposes of the greater self. It does so simply by asking within. When faced with a choice or a decision, for each option it asks the greater self: is this your intent and purpose? The greater self will always signal the correct choice or decision by issuing a yes or no to the story self. It is the job of the story self to discern how the yes or no message has been conveyed. Perhaps it is a word within the mind that seems to be spoken, a whispered yes or no, or a sign will follow that gives confirmation to one of the choices or dissuades from one of the choices. The story self must remain alert to this information.

Living in this way is very relaxing for the story-you, as your job is to simply interpret the messages of the greater you, check in with the greater you for yes and no responses when choices are presented, and act on the desires that arise within your heart. Let us be very specific here. When we say act on the desires of the heart, we mean the positive, constructive, life-affirming desires or feelings that arise and seem to ask that you do a certain thing or that you wait to act, or not act at all. These feelings or desires are otherwise known as feelings of motivation or inspiration.

Feelings of motivation or inspiration often spur you on to take a certain action. They are the steam that runs the engine of your train. In the absence of steam, your greater self is instructing you not to take that action at that time. You know that phrase, "running out of steam." Sometimes a person seems to lose interest, or becomes discouraged about their choices, not finding interest or meaning in the opportunities that confront them. That person is being asked to wait or has not yet learned to focus attention and act on the inner messages of the greater self.

When a person seems to "lose heart," they are feeling a lack of desire or motivation related to a loss of hope. If the energy is not there to move forward because of running out of steam or losing heart, the job of the story self is to 'fall back and punt.' In other words, await new inspiration and direction.

For story characters unaware of the messages of their higher self, the default program tends to elicit unconscious, driven behavior, otherwise known as being proactive. This type of behavior is usually rewarded by the culture, yet it is just another example of the default program which is designed to limit and restrict in all conceivable forms.

While this driven behavior, the urgent need to do something when the character does not know what to do, is simply a program, sometimes it signals an instruction to the aware player from the Godself. In that instance, it will be accompanied by strong motivation and/or feelings of excitement and inspiration. But most urgent action, i.e., steps taken in a consciousness of 'press,' result from automated programs.

When a story character awakens to its presence within a virtual reality or dream reality and to the existence of its greater self, the story character needs only wait for clear instructions from its Godself in the form of inspiration, motivation or events that present themselves. As their consciousness merges with their Godself, they experience themself as customizing the default software.

Every realization of truth results in a customization of the software to encompass that truth. Eventually the software can be redesigned sufficiently to allow a story character to fully access the intents and purposes of its greater self, at which time it experiences itself as the greater self. There are no differences between what it wants and what the greater self wants.

What does it feel like when the story character knows itself to be the greater self? The story, including its sets and supporting characters, takes on a surreal aura. The story character feels the energetic presence of its greater self as being its own form and awareness, and simultaneously being the form and awareness of everything in its moment by moment reality. In other words, the story character walks inside the Godself and is lived by the Godself. The Godself is recognized as the all that is of that story world, the substance of all form. This recognition is uplifting to the story self and makes each moment experienced within the Godself as the greatest moment of their life.

Eventually, the story self wants to feel the presence of the Godself as much as possible, which is when their path of awakening while in the story begins in earnest.

Chapter 4

AWAKENING IN THE STORY

The problems of life as you see it are really problems of loving yourself. When you truly understand the nature of reality, you know that you created every seeming fact of your reality as your greater self, and that your story self supplies the interpretation of those facts. Minus the interpretation of the facts, everything that constitutes your life—your relationships, your finances, your body and your environment—is created by your true self down to the tiniest detail.

However there is one important point to be recognized here. As factual as your reality seems, there is nothing real about it. The facts can change in an instant to support a new reality created by your true self. Your true self, the true part of you, the greater part of you, creates your reality and that reality changes when the greater part of you decides to change it. That is another fact. And since the greater part of you is the same as the story-you, by taking responsibility for the facts, you align with the greater part of you. That alignment creates a difference in your interpretation which then affects your relationship to the greater part of you.

Not loving yourself is a symptom of lack of alignment with the greater part of you and that lack of alignment leads to further perceptions of discrepancy between what you think about your reality and the way it is. The key to moving on, or the automatic transformer of circumstance, is your active alignment with the creator part of you and your active embracing of the reality you find yourself to be in. When resistance to your reality dissolves, reality transforms automatically.

Automatic Transformation

Many times, story selves fear the dissolution of even undesired realities because they know that lack of resistance will cause automatic transformation. What they really fear is the unknown. What will the automatic transformation bring? Will it be something even less desirable than what they had? Will it be something equally challenging to what they had, a challenge that seemed to exhaust and drain them in meeting it. These are not joyful thoughts and will not inspire motivation or inspiration to transform reality. Therefore, you have two factors preventing the automatic transformation of your reality. One is the resistance to the current facts. The second is fear of the unknown of the transformed reality.

These are powerful forces keeping story players on the default path and keeping them from lifting up to alignment with their greater self and fully embracing the story designed by the greater self.

Is the transformed story always a happy one? We have said before that the greater self has its own intents and purposes and seeks to explore its own consciousness in every way imaginable via innumerable expressions of self in innumerable forms of reality. The interpretation of many events in these stories could be viewed as not happy. However, these are only interpretations by the story self.

Events are neither happy nor unhappy. When viewing a movie, do you judge events? You usually go with the flow and have the whole experience, good and bad. It may appear real as far as movies go, but it is not happening to the real you, therefore it is 'only a movie.'

The hardest thing for a story self to grasp is the idea that their life is 'only a movie.' It is not happening to the real you, it is not permanent, lasting or impacting in any way to the real you other than to provide a storehouse of experience and all the sensory data that offers.

For example, when an undesired situation arises in your environment, remind yourself that it is simply a fact. Drop the interpretation that this fatally impacts your health, your work, your flow, your time or your higher purpose, etc., and relax.

There is no event in your outer reality that can actually alter the story that your greater self has designed for you. There is nothing that can harm you in the story or prevent you or stop you, unless that is exactly what your greater self wishes to explore in your experience. A radical detachment from the story is being asked here. And this is the great teaching of Automatic Transformation.

When radical detachment occurs, resistance dissolves to both the current reality and the future reality or transformed reality. When radical detachment occurs, your hypotheses about how your life should have been drop away. There is a silence that overtakes your soul. All you hear are the simple directives of spirit fueled by a feeling of inclination—go here, go there, do this, do that.

You are being called to live without emotional embellishment of your experience. This is the lifestyle of enlightenment and a worthy goal to be sure. Many would bristle at the thought of releasing their emotional responses to events. But when they understand that emotional responses are solely a result of interpretations of story events, the things you tell yourself about what is showing up in the dream around you, they realize that emotional responses are arbitrary, are conditioned, are programmed and have nothing to do with reality. Reality, as defined here, is the stark events orchestrated by your greater self in a virtual story run for the story-you.

You might ask, when alignment with the greater self occurs and acceptance of what-is dominates, what is the nature of the automatic transformation of the story that occurs? Implied here is the idea that the story takes on a tone more favorable to the wishes and desires of the story-you.

Automatic transformation does not always mean the new story or new reality improves upon the old. It is simply a new stage within which new explorations can be launched. Often, however, it is perceived as an improvement by the story self.

Implicit here is the programmed concept that 'life gets better as you go along.' This is not always the case. The idea of something 'getting better,' is a judgment and an interpretation. Again, there are only events, stark factual events, occurring within a dream. There is then your interpretation, or the things you tell yourself or believe to be true about these events. Does that mean that events get better as your life progresses or that automatic transformation means a 'better life?' No. it simply means that the canvas changes and new adventures ensue.

For the story self, an element of courage must be built, the courage to accept what-is, the courage to accept automatic transformation, the courage to not interpret events or have to know what they mean, the courage to live a life that may be far different than the images in the mind of the story self.

Courage is the power to live with dignity whatever the story brings and to not resist transformation because of fear of what the story may bring. Ultimately, after all, the story will bring the ultimate transformation—your exit from the story, and all the details leading up to and comprising that experience. So how can you interpret your life as always improving, as transformation always bringing you into a better story, when you face the ultimate transformation into the unknown of death?

You may decide to interpret this final transformation as a positive one, and therefore view your transformations as positively leading to the ultimate positive—death. In this point of view, your transformation always means a better story. But from another point of view, your transformations always lead to a deepening of the unknown until the final transformation into the unknown.

Which point of view holds the greatest value for a story self? Neither. We are here to tell you that your life is just a movie. You are the greater self watching the show and also experiencing yourself as the lead actor in the show. None of it has any lasting or permanent reality. None of it has any lasting or permanent meaning to the story-you. The only meaning it has is what you tell yourself, and you have the freedom to attribute whatever meaning to the story you wish.

Ultimately, you are in the hands of your greater self, the real you of you, and its own intents and purposes. If you simply make it your goal to align with the intents and purposes of your own greater self and not interpret your experience, and just go along for the ride, whatever it may bring, you will be inviting maximum transformation and maximum opportunity for new adventures.

You now may be wondering, can my adventures be limited by the story self's resistance to change or fear of change? No, the changes will always occur on time, but the story self will have a different quality of experience.

What is the game, but a game of quality of experience. When you align with the highest within you the quality of your experience is felt in the higher octaves of your being, the octaves that ring with presence of God and the implicit joy and bliss of that awareness.

Automatic Transformation seems to suggest that more transformation or more story events can occur if the story self relinquishes its resistance to what-is and fear of what will be. That is not true. The transformations scheduled for the story always occur on schedule. But the self in the story lives out a drama that makes of these transformations and the events leading up to them or following them what it chooses.

The story always plays out on schedule in the same way that a video of a movie always plays out in the correct order of events created for that movie. As in the story, you may make what you choose out of the events in the movie and have whatever response to those events you desire.

Heralds of Change

Subjectively, automatic transformation is made known to the story-you when resistance to what-is is released and fear of what will be is released. That is because, before every change comes a release of resistance and fear. It is a design of the story, a design of the software if you please, that release of resistance to what-is and of fear of what will be heralds the change that has been scheduled in that story.

You cannot rush transformation or manipulate the story. Then what can you do about the undesired aspects of your life? You can use these words to remind yourself that transformation is preceded by the release of resistance to what-is and the release of fear of what will be.

Chapter 5

THE TRUE NATURE OF TRANSFORMATION

Action that results in a new reality requires the acceptance and embracing of the old reality to be released. You perhaps have never seen action defined in this way, but action is never an initiating experience. It is always an automatic effect of the release of resistance-to-what-is.

Transformation is an automatic result of the release of resistance-to-what-is and the release of fear-of-what-will-be. The herald of transformation is the willingness to both be where you are and leap into the unknown. When that state is achieved, transformation invariably follows.

Here is the great secret. Your lives have already been lived, the story has already run just like the movie you saw yesterday or last week has already run. The story was just a blip on the screen of your greater self's Mind. But the story-you is subjectively experiencing the dream as spread out over a time frame spanning many years. The story already happened and the story is happening at the same time. That is how 'premonitions' are discerned. The greater self allows the story self to access information about the story that already occurred outside of the current time frame.

The greater you knows the story in every detail; it constructed your emotional responses and, in some stories, it constructed your healing or release from certain emotional patterns. It set the events and the transformational energies that accompany them—the release energy, the courage energy. You are already back in the reality of the greater you, watching with the greater you, watching as the greater you, the movie of your story.

Can you change the movie? No. Just as you can't change the movies that run in the theaters of your world, you can't change your story movie. You can, however, create the illusion of change by altering the perspective you take on your experience and by altering what you tell yourself about your experience, which in turn alters the subjective quality of your experience while in the story.

Your greater self has arranged for you to know this information or to read this information, which is a signal to you, the reader, that you have the potential to achieve greater freedom, psychological freedom, within the story, than you have experienced heretofore. You would not be reading this or have continued to this point if you were not seeking freedom from the impact of the events of your reality.

Within your craving to create reality lies the craving for freedom from the impact of interpretations and meanings you give to the events of your reality. These interpretations and meanings are sometimes personal, but more often they are shared by members of your culture, adding further power and impact to these events. If the event is interpreted as negative by you, it is likely viewed as a negative by others in your culture, thus helping you feel as badly as possible about what happened. None of these interpretations have anything to do with reality, which is just the experience of an event that has no need for interpretation or meaning attributed to it.

However, some events are meant to be interpreted a certain way by you, and by your culture, so that your story can take a certain track fueled by the meaning you give to an event that is shared by your culture. In this way causes are taken up and activism may occur. This type of experience has been fully orchestrated by your greater self as are all types of experience. Your emotional responses are also orchestrated by your greater self until the story self starts to question the meaning of events and their interpretation of events.

The default software provides certain basic automated emotional responses to certain types of events as a starting point, aligned always with the culture within which the story-you arises. Attaining freedom in the story is not your freedom from the storyline as it were, but your freedom from these automated emotions and from the meanings and interpretations they are associated with.

Chapter 6

WELCOME TO THE PHYSICAL ILLUSION

What exactly is the default software? Know that there is nothing real in the consciousness of God. Everything is maya—an illusion, including the illusion of realness. There is only consciousness and the spiritual realms of exploration within. Therefore, the idea of default software is simply a convenience, a way of describing the illusion world you find yourself in and the body you are using, not to mention the emotions and thoughts that pepper your day.

In this and the following two chapters, we shall take each aspect of the software one at a time; first your physical world, second your body and third your thoughts and emotions.

The Illusion World

The physical illusion world is a creation of consciousness and has no solidity, no reality and no substance. It has no more reality than the world of your dreams last night, yet it is programmed to be perceived as solid and lasting. It has been programmed to exist within an illusion labeled Time and Space, whereas your dream last night did not have the time and space factor. It simply was. It played out in consciousness. Perhaps it inhabited a place, but everything was experienced as fluid and temporary.

The difference between your dream reality and your physical reality is the illusion of permanence in the latter. Some have dreams that seem to return to the same dream reality and therefore may convey a sense of permanence, as if these locales do remain standing after the dreamer has departed the nighttime sojourn. But that is an illusion within an illusion.

Dream realities are created on the spot so to speak, and there is default software that governs the default nature of dreaming while in the physical illusion world. We will discuss this later.

The software of the physical world is not a thing as you would understand your computer software to be. It is not a construction that is independent of the user. It is simply a thought, but a very complex and layered thought. Nothing in the physical world has substance, much less the software that runs it.

The physical world software is nothing more than a thought in the consciousness of your greater self. This thought contains all the elements of your world, as created and designed within the mind of your greater self. It contains the unique elements customized for your personal Life-Time experience. It contains all the details of the world that seem to exist around you independent of your awareness.

When you sleep at night, you imagine the world continues. When you make your ultimate transformation out of the physical illusion, you imagine your legacy goes on or the world itself goes on without you. If you have children, you imagine your children go on, carrying on your physical genes.

None of this is true. When you exit the illusion, it simply means the software closes down. When you shut down your computer at night along with all of its components, do you imagine its software continues on without you? No, when you shut down your software, it shuts down and figuratively speaking awaits your reopening.

There is no planet earth. There are no children. There is no legacy of money, work or genes. What you experience in the illusion is the sum total of your experience. It begins and ends with your awareness of having this experience.

The software world is made for you, just like a movie is made for its main character. When the film is run on film equipment, the story unfolds for two hours. When it runs to the end, it is then removed from the equipment and put in a can.

The world of the film, the characters of the film, the family of those characters and the implied results or effects of what happened in the story, including what the lead character accomplished or failed to accomplish, do not continue on after the film is put back in the can. And when that roll of film is run again, it is always identical to the first time it was run and will never suddenly sprout new story lines or endings.

Similarly, your movie begins and runs to the end; it is then put aside. What occurred in your dream of a Life-Time ends with the closing down of the software and your return to your greater self. The memories of that experience become encapsulated in the consciousness of your greater self and the value extracted according to the needs and desires of the greater self. There is no independent reality to anything that occurred in your Life-

Time. It does not 'go on' outside of your greater self's consciousness.

The software world you inhabit while playing the Life-Time game is simply a bundled thought in the Mind of your greater self. This software is utilized for other runs of the game with other characters invented by the greater self. However, there is a variation on that world for every era, every phase and every character in the game. The variation is recorded in the thought bundle and becomes a default of the software for that character, that era and that phase of the game.

The greater self of you encodes the software to contain the exact elements it requires for your run. It may run the same characters over and over again in multiple worlds, in order to extract maximum data from a particular character's experience. This is simply according to the desires or wishes of the greater self in its exploration of consciousness and has no further meaning or value. We are saying here that your story character's repeated presence in your greater self's software journeys does not make that character special to the greater self, just useful as it peruses time and space worlds of its own creation.

Imagination is the realm of consciousness. Imagination is, literally, God. Nothing that is takes place outside of the imagination or consciousness of God. God is the greater self of you and everyone else. God is running the infinite numbers of stories in software worlds, stories which seem to overlap, which seem to have lasting value or permanence across time, but which are in actuality just a play of consciousness within the infinite and ever-expanding mind of God.

The past of your illusion world, including the great masterpieces of art, literature, science, architecture, music and theater, is a creation of your own greater self. If you view your world as the doll house or electric train set of your childhood, you may have purchased miniature items to lend tones of reality to that dollhouse or train set. Perhaps you purchased a tiny painting for the wall in the dining room of the dollhouse, or a miniature tree to stand alongside the tracks of your train set. All of this was to add reality to your illusion world, the miniaturized world of a house or train track. In this way, the greater self of you uses its infinite consciousness to decorate the world of your illusions.

Consciousness loves to play in multiple eras simultaneously and loves to create the illusion of arts and sciences through its story characters relevant to that era. It loves to see some of these creations duplicated in the software of other eras where it benefits the story. Hence, if the story takes place in an Amazonian tribe that never experiences the modern world, the presence of these artistic creations is irrelevant and will not be programmed into the default.

However, if a member of that tribe were to venture out of the Amazon, move to the big city and go to a museum, then art would be programmed into the default software of that character's game world. That art might be typical of the region or might be representative of other regions of the world, depending on the intent of the museum experience for that character's story.

The character will always experience precisely what the greater self desires it to experience. The greater self has pre-programmed the software to contain all the needed elements for each phase of the journey.

Does this mean that the greater self creates great art anew for each character's illusion journey? No. The default software contains elements that were once created and are selected for inclusion as part of that character's journey.

Many characters share similar elements in their software, including the common experience of great art and science, such as the works of Mozart or the theories of Darwin. However, great art and science are not created by story characters from the past or by present characters in the self's journey. Only in the illusion is creation of great art or science attributed to story characters of past and present. They are always a creation of your greater self and do not exist independent of the story.

When you realize how great your own greater self is in its ability to create even the most genius aspects of your very own world, not to mention the enormous detail within which this world unfolds for your journey, you can appreciate the extraordinary nature of that consciousness which is your own greater self, the real you of you. You are the great one who is doing all the creating from a place beyond time and space. There is only one you and that is the All That Is, the Absolute, the Creator of all that is.

Does your creator self assign, so to speak, management of certain worlds to lesser creations of itself? In other words, is there a hierarchy of consciousness? Your absolute self has created infinite modes of exploring its own consciousness, including the existence of aspects of itself which run the journeys of characters in various illusion worlds. The greater you is an aspect of the Absolute, just as you are an aspect of the greater you, but ultimately, everything can only be one thing—the Absolute.

Chapter 7

THE PHYSICAL BODY ILLUSION

What is your body but a thought in the Mind of God, or more specifically a default aspect of your physical world software. It has been customized by your greater self according to the specific needs, intents and purposes of your story self during its Life-Time. The body is a representation of you, the main character in your story and is designed to appear solid, real, and three-dimensional.

Is it real? No, it is not real other than in its reality within the context of the software. When the software shuts down at the end of your journey there are no remains, meaning no body is left behind or buried in the ground. The death ritual, including burial rituals, is simply an artifact of the culture within which the Life-Time is being run. The body does not outlast the software. Does your computer software continue to process data when you shut down the computer? The answer, of course, is no.

It is something to behold, when you consider how intricate are the processes governing a physical body in the illusion. Yet none of them are real or have independent existence outside of the software being run. The body contains an elaborate system of organs, arteries, blood, bone and skin that fascinate with their reality. The default software contains beliefs that the body can be destroyed, the body can be damaged, the body can be impaired in any number of ways, and entire medical books are devoted to the microscopic analysis of every bodily constituent.

All of this enormous detail drives home a sense of reality to the body, made most real in its insistent needs for shelter, food and sex, and in its ability to feel pain and pleasure. It is almost impossible for a story character to not believe the body is real, even if they can to some degree convince themself that the world is not real or that they live in a matrix-type of software. Such is the power the body has over your lives.

True freedom begins and ends with freedom from the belief in the body's reality and the understanding of its temporary function in your software excursion. If you did nothing else but focus on freeing yourself from the almost endless cultural programming that purports to help your illusion body, e.g., warns about possible harm to the body, encourages giving pleasure of various kinds to the body or avoiding pain of various kinds to the body, instructs on how to transport the body, decorate the body, clothe and shelter the body, reproduce via the body, entertain the body, educate the body (or, in this case, the brain encased in the body), find friends for the body, find love for the body, find success for the body, obtain money for the survival and comfort of the body, etc., you would be focused in the most powerful way possible.

Through the body is your freedom fast track for those waking up in the dream. And what is it you want freedom from? You want freedom from being trapped in an illusion that locks you into the default program. By awakening to the body illusion, your ability to customize the program increases exponentially. The potential is unlimited when you grasp the complete non-reality of your body and are unmoved by its appearance, its seeming health or lack thereof, and the drives that course through it on a near-constant basis.

Detachment from the body's illusion needs and ailments is often sufficient to the goal of achieving freedom, for when you work with the body, you work at the core of the software, at the heart of survival issues. This is, in some sense, what the Indian fakirs hint at when they remain poised in a certain position for hours on end, appearing to transcend the limits or needs of the body. It is not to prove to you that you have to develop your body to the point of super-strength, but to show you there are no limits, and the body is just an illusion.

Many interpret the messages and signs scattered in your world on a daily basis as being an impetus to building up the body in some way, improving the body in some way. But every time the body's health or well being is referenced in your culture, it can be viewed as a moment to remind yourself that the body is not real; it is simply an illusion created by your own greater self, the true you.

Take time to sense during your day how you are actually a consciousness that appears to use a body to create, for example, this manuscript, or to do anything else you may choose to do in your daily life.

The key word is 'appears.' You appear to use a body. The truth is, the body is an illusion created by the software. The 'you' that experiences itself as 'inside' this body is an extension of your greater self. Since the illusion software is nothing less than a complex thought in the mind of God, all components of the illusion, including your body, are nothing less than a complex thought in the mind of God. Your body is an idea, a reference point for the greater self's extension so that the greater self can experience itself at the center of the Life-Time experience.

What is the meaning of body as illusion and how do you free yourself from its many limitations? First, understand that these limitations are customizations of the illusion software courtesy of your greater self. They serve a purpose known only to the greater self. In every case, however, they serve the story and have meaning only in relation to the intents and purposes of your greater self for this Life-Time journey experience. Your job is not to question the presence of these customizations. Even when they appear to be painful or disabling, they have been created by your greater self for its own intents and purposes. And even though you may be in pursuit of solutions to your illusion physical issues, know that this seeking of solutions and your seeming failure or success are all part of your Life-Time storyline.

When you awaken to the non-reality of your body and your presence as consciousness having an illusion of being in a body with a world unfolding around it, you can customize the software to your liking. At that point in your awareness, you may choose to change or not change the current physical illusion you are experiencing. For once the intents and purposes of your greater self are known, the intents and purposes of the character in the story change.

At the core of the physical illusion experience is the experience of being in the illusion of a physical body. Therefore, many of the sensations, needs, seeming problems or limitations of the body are natural to the physical illusion. Your journey is a physical world journey. True, it is an illusion of such, but it is designed with tones of reality down to the tiniest detail. The seeming limitations of your body are part of these tones of reality that enable the greater you to focus in the dream. It desires to have a complete physical world experience. Therefore, the software is designed to give the illusion of a physical world with all of its problems and limitations.

Physical by definition implies temporary, deteriorating, with a beginning and an ending. Nothing physical can be permanent, nothing physical remains the same. There is constant entropy, and the law of entropy within the default program creates the heaviness and all the other discomforts of the physical.

While in a physical illusion, you can never be completely free of the discomforts of being physical. If you were, it would not be a physical illusion. However, when you enter the portal, find that narrow doorway to freedom, you are able to experience both the presence of your greater self and the presence of your physical illusion body simultaneously. The identification with your greater self enables you to experience your body as a sensory apparatus that can be adjusted and customized to a great extent.

The greater your identification with your greater self the more ability you have to override the defaults governing the body. However, there are certain basic components of the software that cannot be overruled in this particular illusion. These include defying gravity, walking on water, going through walls, etc. Because the physical is designed to be solid and feel solid, these attributes cannot be accessed from the physical. While there really are no rules, the greater self sets parameters for a physical journey which most of the time do not allow for those types of experiences. They can, however, be accessed in other states of consciousness while in the physical, states labeled out of body, astral travel and dreaming.

Let us look at the issue that comes up over and over again: how can your greater self cause so much pain and sorrow? When you suffer in the body, you feel trapped in the physical world, and its nature as illusion is more distant than ever. This raises the opportunity to vanquish the illusion once and for all. For when you confront the dis-ease in your body as illusion and trust that you are consciousness having this dream of limitation in the body, and actually feel how you are both consciousness and a body in an illusion of limitation, a doorway opens.

Transformation is imminent when you have achieved realization of the truth of your situation. When you can look ahead and not fear the unknown, transformation is guaranteed. We will discuss later how to arrive at this stage in your awareness as quickly as possible.

Chapter 8

YOUR THOUGHTS AND EMOTIONS

The default software for your physical illusion Life-Time experience is pre-installed with a wide range of beliefs and emotional responses to those beliefs. That is how your world seems to reflect back to you so many of these beliefs and their concomitant emotional responses. You are mostly a ping pong ball, bouncing from thought or belief to emotion, then back to thought or belief, then back to emotion, ad infinitum. Your entire day is spent as a ping pong ball which is being bounced so to speak by the software program.

Yet all of your reactions feel sincere and ever so real, and all your thoughts so meaningful and believable. This is the part of the program that finds innumerable ways to lend tones of reality to your experience down to the tiniest detail. So what you view as your feelings, your thoughts, your beliefs, your opinions, your ideas, are simply default programs of the software.

There is no individuality in the illusion except that which has been pre-installed as part of the customization of your story. Your greater self conceives of the total you, the story it will experience, and the qualities in you that will be needed to explore certain aspects of consciousness in the context of this story. Those qualities are the customized beliefs, thoughts and emotions, as well as the specific drives, desires and dreams you come in with or which appear to surface spontaneously at predetermined stages of the journey.

These thoughts, emotions, drives, desires and dreams are the fuel for your journey. The software provides the body, the setting and the illusion of other players. If you understand that thoughts, emotions, drives, desires and dreams take place in consciousness, you can see that your greater self is the part of you driving these customized facets of your story self's consciousness. By grasping the meaning of that understanding, you can align with the greater self and trust in the process.

Your greater self creates your reality down to the tiniest detail. Yet there is a powerful program in the default software causing you to believe that your 'subconscious' is 'sabotaging' you and that 'subconscious beliefs' are creating the problems in your world. This program causes you to feel at effect to your own subconscious and to the beliefs held there without your knowledge or control. It further teaches that by visualizing the opposite, or accessing the 'negative' beliefs and 'dis-creating' them or substituting a positive belief you are then free of this sabotage and free to live the life of your dreams.

That training is not the truth; rather, the default of your software has been customized to accept these 'new age' conditionings. You are being asked to go beyond the new age conditioned thought. The information in this book scales mountains beyond new age thought.

Relax, rest in our words. We will show you a way, a truth, a knowledge, that is the greatest joy you have ever known, for you will have the truth of your soul, the truth by which you may live in a state of freedom rarely attained by a story character.

The author's dream is a dream of freeing all the characters in the story, a dream of teaching them freedom and truth. The author's motto: the truth shall set you free.

Your default program contains innumerable beliefs and their concomitant illusion appearances and results. For example, it will send you in search of success, if that is significant to your story, weighed down by a truckload of beliefs that will trigger emotional responses to the events of your journey. When confronting the illusion of delay, rejection or failure, you will have the automatic response of frustration, anger and dejection. When confronting success you will have the automatic response of relief, joy and feeling temporarily 'high.'

It is that temporary 'high' that drives the persistent craving for success, like a drug high drives the craving to locate it, purchase it and take it. Success is both a legal high in your culture as well as a default program of your software. Its addictive quality ensures your continued pursuit.

It is important to see here that when you don't know that you are a great, infinite being having a blip in time journey as an illusion person in an illusion world, you are controlled completely by the default software. You allow the software to dictate your emotions, your actions and your beliefs. You judge others and the world around you according to these same emotions, actions and beliefs. It is a dog chasing its tail experience, the true meaning of 'going around in circles.' Yet this is how the overwhelming majority spends their entire lives.

I am here to tell you that there is a way out of the fully conditioned way of life you are awakening from. To find that doorway, you must have the passion in your heart for truth and freedom. That passion is either given to you by your greater self as a customized pattern, so that you can make this discovery or attempt to, or it is not. If you have read up to this point and are still with us, you have likely been given the passion for truth and freedom that will enable you to find the doorway.

Once the doorway is found, not all of you will choose to walk through. For those who reach the door but do not open it, your greater self has allowed only partial awakening for its own intents and purposes. There is nothing wrong with this, as there is nothing wrong with any of the many software journeys run by the greater self. Only certain of these journeys allow a story character to venture through the portal. As always, your greater self designs each journey for its own intents and purposes in its ongoing exploration of consciousness.

By the end of this book, you will understand how to find the doorway, and how to go through the portal. But it is up to you to choose whether to go through or not. When you go through the portal, you will experience reality as a dream, you will dream it in alignment with your greater self and as your greater self, you will be free of the default emotions and beliefs of the software program, and you will know an internal freedom while still within the journey that makes of your life a glorious adventure.

Chapter 9

THE PEACE THAT PASSETH UNDERSTANDING

What is the peace that passeth understanding but a surrender to the truth of your actual circumstance as a story character in a virtual world created by your greater self for its own intents and purposes. Peace comes when you realize that you can never know what anything means or what anything is. You can only know what the default program instructs you to know, echoed by your culture and the belief system of everyone you relate to.

The culture does not program you—you arrive pre-programmed with the default program. As mentioned before, it contains the unique customization suited to your life journey and the potential for further customization along the way. When you achieve total alignment with your greater self, who is the creator and observer of you—its extension within the virtual world it has created—you gain the freedom to customize as your greater self.

You do not become a wild card, running off with the program so to speak in any direction the story-you desires. You become your greater self, fully self aware in the program, and living with the consciousness of your greater self as your consciousness in the virtual world. You will discover in so doing that the consciousness of your greater self has its own intents and purposes, its own unconditioned way of viewing your life and your experiences, and these intents and purposes and perspectives become your own.

Does this mean that awakening fully to your situation and aligning fully with your higher self allows you to fulfill all your dreams and desires? This is an individual determination. You may realize that many of your dreams and desires were programs, conditioned dreams and desires that have no further bearing on your life. You may discover new dreams and desires, those of your greater self, and joyfully proceed to fulfill them. Or, your awakened self may find that within the story character's dreams and desires are the kernel of the true dreams and desires of the true self. That kernel will sprout into full bloom within the consciousness of being your greater self in the story.

Many of your desires and dreams in the story world are default programs echoed by the culture, seemingly instilled by the culture, but actually just reflected by the culture and the world around you. They are not the true desires and dreams of the greater you, who has its own intents and purposes, perhaps light years away from what you understand to be your purpose. Your job as an extension in the virtual world is to detach from what you believe to be your intents and purposes and constantly orient to your greater self and ask, is this *Your* intent and purpose? Once full alignment is achieved, that question need never be repeated as the extension then knows fully what is being asked of it. The desires of the greater self stripped of the default programs become the desires of the extension and in this way there can never be a failure to fulfill a dream or desire.

Desires and dreams may seem to not be fulfilled or to not 'come true.' When the perception of those desires and dreams are so distorted by the extension due to the default program and the cultural mirrors, there can only be one true goal for that extension—to wake up to the intents and purposes, the dreams and desires of the true self. Those dreams and desires are free of conditioning, have been customized by the software for your access upon awakening, and simply await your activation. They can never be met with anything but success.

True success is the freedom to create your reality in alignment with the true desires and dreams of your greater self. That freedom to create is a result of your awakening to your true condition within the virtual world and to your true nature as an extension of an infinite being. Once you fully understand the nature of your reality, you are free. The truth sets you free. It sets you free to express the intents and purposes of your greater self while in the story. There is never a time too early or too late, or an age too young or too old, to discover and awaken to the intents and purposes of your greater self. That awakening is always customized in your story by your greater self and happens on schedule. If there is no awakening, it is not in your story.

For those drawn to these teachings, there is an awakening customized for your story that awaits your alignment with your greater self. The clearer your understanding of the nature of your personal reality in the virtual world, the easier it is to let go of resistance to 'what-is' and fear of 'what will be.' In that moment, the door opens and the story character slips into the customized world of living in alignment with the intents and purposes of the true self.

The keys to your awakening are understanding the nature of reality, recognizing that your unfulfilled dreams and desires are not aligned with your greater self's intents and purposes, understanding the elements of automatic transformation, and acquiring the willingness to surrender to the true desires and dreams of your greater self for your character's Life-Time. Mastering each of these elements will be discussed in detail later in this book.

Once truly awakened, you realize exactly what your greater self wishes to experience through you, the extension, and you give the greater self what it asks. Life becomes extraordinarily simple. When doubt arises, you need only ask within, "Is this Your intent and purpose?"

Everything in your world is there because of your greater self. Everything. And that includes the events and situations that seem to push you to the edge of your tolerance, that seem untenable, that make of life a nightmare. In those moments, you are being asked to know the truth. Each time those moments occur you have another opportunity to embrace the truth. If you do, you will find yourself lifted into a new reality.

What is that truth but the recognition that this is a scene created by your own greater self. It is a scene in a movie within which you find yourself a lead character. It is a scene that seems to threaten your well being or security in some way, otherwise it would not have the power to disturb you to the extent it does.

These scenes are set ups from your greater self. They are designed to uproot you from your programs and conditioned patterns. The more intense are these scenes, the more powerfully you are being lifted out of your default software and the greater the potential to customize your future. Bottom line, these are gifts from your greater self.

We know that this seems like the last thing these difficult moments and scenarios are, but we assure you they are the greatest gifts you can receive, because they will, if viewed as such, liberate you to an extent unimaginable to your default self.

When receiving this gift in the midst of the drama, take a moment to recognize it is a gift. That inner acknowledgement gives you a bit of detachment that even though small allows you to carry out the gift's intent and purpose. And what is that? Simply, it is there to help you acknowledge that you are in a movie; you are a lead character; the situation confronting you is a creation of your greater self which is the infinite you of you. It is therefore created by you for your own intents and purposes.

The question that must be asked is what is your intent and purpose with this scenario? What is being asked of me in the story? In the act of listening for an answer will come your answer. This is an automatic part of the software program. When you orient to your greater self, you will always hear from the part of you that is objectively observing your story.

It is an undeniable aspect of your story that the most painful moments and scenarios are the greatest opportunities for power and freedom within the story. This is hard to accept when living those moments which appear to consume your thoughts and emotions. But just intending to inject a bit of distance into the moment when the scenario repeats itself, as it will, and then ask the question inwardly of your greater self, you will find the gift of that moment in the answer.

When you receive an answer, you must act on it. The answer of the moment is always the correct answer. Interpreting its meaning requires your willingness to know the truth of your greater self and its intents and purposes. Living out the meaning requires your willingness to follow through on the intents and purposes of your greater self. You can never make a mistake in so doing, for you are rewarded in each moment you allow your consciousness to be directed by the greater part of you, even when your connection with that part appears to be impaired or inaccurate.

Just the intent to engage with your greater self during those moments that challenge you to the utmost enables the power of your greater self to become active in the story through you. Do not make the mistake of underestimating the power of your greater self to guide you through the most difficult moments of your life. You are never without the help you need, never alone in a cold, uncaring world, never abandoned by loved ones or without answers to your most pressing problems.

All of this is a creation of your greater self so you will come to your senses during the story and recognize that you are in a story and can thereby customize your software as the greater self of you. This is accomplished through orienting toward the intents and purposes of your greater self and allowing It to direct your story character.

When your story character is fully aligned with its true self, it lives as the greater self in the story and needs fear nothing. For the greater self is the creator of the story, the power behind the story, and the infinite, indestructible part of you.

How do you know you are aligning with the greater self? Simply make the effort, when feeling disturbed about anything in your world. Right in the midst of your pain and fear, inwardly remind yourself of your true situation. Inwardly remember who you really are and what is really happening—just a story character in a movie.

When events appear to come at you hard and fast and there seems to be no time to remember the truth, use the command, "Truth." By declaring truth inwardly, you will suddenly find a path of light opens and your way out will become immediately apparent.

Try this at every opportunity, particularly when beset by an insoluble problem. Truth is your savior, for the truth always sets you free. Be willing to know the truth, free of your preconceptions and programs.

The greater you of you will always tell you the truth about your situation and will show the perfect path for you to tread. It happens in an instant; that is the gift and the blessing you are always entitled to in every moment, in every situation. Command to know the truth, dear reader, and the truth shall set you free of your difficulty.

When in the midst of an argument, the recurring arguments between yourself and the difficult loved ones in your life, cry out inwardly for Truth, and you will find a new perspective and new way of being in the midst of strife. You must try this in order to prove the power of this simple technique.

You are gifted with this technique because your greater self always responds to a story character seeking to communicate with it and to know the big picture, the truth of its situation and the intents and purposes of the greater self.

If you are committed to freeing yourself from the illusion of being a physical body in a physical world, cry out to your greater self for Truth at every opportunity and you will be lifted into a new world before your very eyes. Look forward to these opportunities when they come, as they enable you to test this technique.

The more you use it, the greater are the changes you will experience within yourself that lift you into the consciousness of your greater self. When this alignment achieves ignition, or critical mass, your story transforms automatically. For in the seeking of Truth, is embodied the willingness to release your resistance to what-is and your fear of what will be. Thus, automatic transformation unfolds in your experience and you are lifted into the magical life of your greater self.

How is the life of your greater self a magical life? When the intents and purposes of your greater self are being lived by you, consciously, joyously, and fully, there can only be a magical life. It is a life you were designed for, the ultimate version of the software movie you inhabit as lead character. It is the most fulfilled possible life, even if you would never have believed it before your transformation.

And do not assume it is only one transformation. The ultimate and final transformation to oneness with your higher self is the result of innumerable smaller transformations. They are reflections, each and every time, of your willingness to let go of your definition of the truth and allow the greater self to instruct you. The ultimate and final transformation is cumulative and places you firmly in the presence of your greater self who now walks as the virtual you of your storyline.

Chapter 10

RIDING THE STORYLINE

The ultimate storyline experience is to surrender to the greater self and trust in the greater self's intents and purposes. It will never lead you astray. It will always raise you into a self and a version of the storyline which reflects the most exalted potentialities for your Life-Time.

Each character's story exists in a vibrational range or frequency range reflective of the consciousness imbued in that story character. When the consciousness of that character is fully aligned with its greater self, the story vibrates octaves higher, bringing a wholly new storyline into view that would have never been possible before.

Each frequency upgrade a story character allows, by orienting toward the intents and purposes of its greater self, most especially during the moments of greatest challenge and pain, raises the character's storyline and alters its trajectory.

There is the default story, as previously mentioned, and the exalted story, which is the ultimate potential of a fully Self-realized character.

The truth is that there is nothing that can harm you, only the illusion of harm. There is no reason for harm to come to you ever. Only your confusion by the illusion creates the storyline where harm may seem to come. Harm never comes. Remember who you are: an illusion of a person in a body in a physical world.

Can anything harm an illusion? Were you harmed in your dreams last night? The physical illusion is no different than the world of your dreams and has no further impact on, or power over, the real you. Nothing that occurs in the illusion is real, dear reader, including the illusion that harm ever occurred or can occur.

This is the hardest thing for story characters to grasp, as the sensation of pain and suffering blocks the awareness of illusion. But just like awakening in a lucid dream enables you to control the dream—such that the pain you may feel in that dream, or the impending danger, dissolve when you view it with lucidity or when you simply wake up—so does the lucid consciousness of the story character in the illusion physical world awaken to the truth that nothing ever happened to it, nothing ever threatened it, nothing was ever real. It was just a movie in the mind of its greater self, played out within certain parameters and designed by the greater self.

You are the greater self of you and cannot be destroyed, ever. You cannot be harmed, you cannot be limited, you cannot be betrayed, you cannot be made small. Only the illusion of such can possess your story self, and merely awaits your recognition of Truth to be put out.

I hear you ask, but remembering who I am in the story doesn't change anything. I have this pain or that, this problem or that, and everything stays the same, even when I cry out for truth and remember I am a greater self in an illusion story.

Say to yourself now, I am the creator of this story. I am the creator of this illusion person in this illusion story. I am designing this story so that this illusion person can remember it is Me. When this illusion person stops being mesmerized by the illusion and remembers it is Me, I reward it by lifting it up into a higher octave of its story. This plays out as magical events seeming to relieve this illusion person of its illusion challenges.

Remember, dear one, there is the default and there is the 'exalt.' The default contains all the limitations you have fully explored thus far. If you are reading this book, you are seeking the 'exalt.'

Choose the exalted consciousness now. Say, "I choose the exalted consciousness. I choose the consciousness of my greater self. Even though I appear to be this troubled, weak, miserable and vulnerable person in this story, I choose to be exalted as my greater self."

Say this aloud now:

I choose to be exalted as my greater self.

I choose the consciousness of my greater self.

I am my greater self.

My greater self is the creator of my story.

I am the creator of my story as my greater self.

My greater self and I are one and the same.

The idea that I am separate from my greater self is an illusion that helped me live the default story.

The recognition that I am actually my greater self, who is extended into this story as an illusion persona, enables me to live the exalted story.

I am willing now to live the exalted story.

I embrace the exalted story.

I allow the exalted story.

I give up all my ideas about how my life should look.

I allow everything happening in my life to be as it is without worrying or concerning myself about anything.

I allow everything that ever seemed to happen in my life to fade into the nothingness from which it came and I allow it be without worry or concern.

I am the Exalted Self.

I am the consciousness of my exalted self living now my exalted life.

I am lifted now into the highest octave possible for this Life-Time.

I am willing for this transformation to alter every aspect of my life and body according to its parameters.

I surrender completely to the highest story possible in this experience.

I am the highest me possible in this experience.

I am indestructible, eternal, permanent and unlimited.

I am the Exalted Self in extension here in this Life-Time.

My Life-Time illusion experience is now under full control and direction by the highest octaves of the software.

My default software is now customized at the highest possible level.

Only magical events can follow this transformation to my exalted Life-Time.

I do not judge what seems to be. I do not fear what seems to happen. I do not worry about anything.

I trust that I am now living my exalted Life-Time as the highest me of me, aligned fully with my greatest self.

I live with the full power of my greatest self imbuing me to be all that It desires me to be.

I let go of thinking I know anything about how this magical life should look.

I let go of judging the others in my magical life and of thinking I know anything about how they should look or act.

I am at peace in the consciousness of my greater self.

I am at peace living the magical life of my exalted self.

I am in joy and appreciation of my exalted self and the magical life I now live.

I now call everything magical, and live in total joy and appreciation.

I now call myself exalted and live in total joy and appreciation of myself.

I love my life in every aspect and trust it is all good.

I appreciate my greater self for giving me this gift of expanded consciousness.

I love my expanded consciousness and my realization that I am the exalted self of me.

I love my exalted life.

I love my exalted self.

I love any remnants of my old life that may still appear to be in my story.

I love and trust that whatever remnants of my old storyline are there for reasons that serve me as the exalted self in my higher octave story.

I love and trust that there are higher and higher octaves to this story that I continually expand into.

I love and trust this ever expanding process and allow it to unfold exactly as my exalted self wishes it to unfold in accordance with its intents and purposes.

I strive to live the intents and purposes of my exalted self and orient to its instructions and inner guidance at all times.

I live fully aligned with my exalted self and allow my exalted self to enter my persona and uplift my storyline.

I am the greater Me now.

Thank God for that!

The above declarations should be made daily. They should be the first thing you remind yourself of when you wake up. Simply read aloud these declarations. They will immediately raise your vibration to the highest and allow your exalted self to connect with your persona and embody it.

Chapter 11

PLAYING A NEW GAME

From this high state of consciousness arises the idea of a new game that is more powerful than any other game out there; more fun, more effective, more exalting, more joyful, more enlivening, more expansive, more abundance producing and more creativity enhancing than anything out there; more love enhancing, more pleasure enhancing, more power enhancing, the power to create, to be all of me, to have all I choose. It is the choosing game; the game of choose and receive, the game of command and receive. And God said, let there be light!

And there was light! The game where all you do is say what you want and the result, if it's a physical issue, is instantaneous healing. If it's a financial healing, then the means for this healing arrives virtually immediately—in no more than 72 hours. If the healing is needed by twelve o'clock tonight, it arrives by twelve o'clock tonight. That is what is specified in the command.

There is no waiting, no waiting on the gods to reorganize the ethers to bring together your result, to create the right conditions. The right conditions manifest upon conception and verbalization of the request. The two are instantaneous and automatic.

The creation of opportunity is always immediate, meaning the opportunity that provides the desired result. All that is needed is a clearly expressed choice. Then one must act on the opportunity. This is a way to move your life along quickly into desired channels—the end of pain, the end of suffering here and now. It's where you begin with yourself. But there are several things you must ask for first in order to 'format your disc' so to speak. And they must be asked in the correct way.

Once your disc is formatted, you may then make one command per day of what you most desire. There must be an order to these commands. They must begin with your having all the incomplete and disturbing conditions in your life transformed. Meaning, you begin with transforming the residual of your previous game.

Everything currently showing up in your world is a residual of the previous game. Some of it you wish to keep, at least for the time being, other of it you wish to excise or otherwise transform. You must make a list of what you wish to transform and what you wish to transform it into. You do not specify people to play specific roles. You allow the people to appear for those roles. They may already be in your life, suddenly deciding to play a new role, or they may be completely new.

New actors coming on the stage are always related to the commands put into motion. You must record your commands. You must record your results. One page per command. You do not request other people to change EVER. You simply describe the scenario you wish to experience with another person. That is your one command for that day. Each year you may make 365 commands.

Commands must be made in the morning and the result tracked at night. If the command has not brought a result by night, the command is made again. There must be a sense of absolute certainty behind the command. The command is made for things that appear to be difficult for you to have but which you must have in order to have peace, joy or full self expression. In other words, do not make a command for something you can just walk down to the grocery store and buy.

And again, you can never make a command that a certain person changes in this or that way or does this or that thing. Commands must address the general issue.

For example, if you have a disobedient teen, you don't command that the teen starts to listen and obey and stops running around at all hours with friends. You command that a healing of your relationship with that teen now takes place for the highest good of both of you.

When you make the command it now must be so. It's that you did not notice you were God, creating all the time. Write down the command. Speak it aloud with conviction. Watch for your receiving. By the end of the day record your observations, noting the slightest signs that show positive change in the relationship.

Perhaps these signs are in your own feelings, a more accepting feeling towards your teen, or a more loving or positive attitude towards your teen. And perhaps your teen is showing more consideration or politeness to you. Whatever results you notice, look for even the tiniest change in yourself or in the teen and record it.

The next morning, make a new command and record it on a fresh page. It could be something small, related to the previous matter or completely different. It could relate to things you have neglected to finish or resisted taking care of. Or perhaps you felt you couldn't afford a certain thing which is why it was neglected.

You must fashion your command as God would. You are god of your own reality in a dream world, a quantum world, where anything goes, anything can happen instantaneously.

Let us say that your next command is to complete the cleaning out of the garage, a chore you procrastinated for years, but which upsets you whenever you think about it or go into the garage. How would you format that command—remember as God, an old reality blinks out and a new reality blinks in, it is as easy as that.

In your imagination, visualize the garage. You are holding a magic wand with a ball of light sparkling brilliantly at the end. You are a gigantic entity, looking down at a tiny messy garage. You strike your magic wand on it and declare, "Abracadabra, garage you are now in order rapidly and effortlessly."

Imagine a blinding light striking your garage, and when it fades you are now looking at a completely orderly space. Don't focus on detail, just the general appearance, from a distance, as a gigantic genie, or angel, or godlike entity, whatever you wish.

Now you go about your day, noticing if any urges arise that take you into the garage to clean it up, or if you get an idea, such as how you could hire someone, e.g., neighborhood kids, to do it for you or help you. Take action as you are guided. At the end of the day, write down anything you noticed about this command. If necessary make your command again. Then let it go.

For physical ailments, visualize two burning wands of light on the area from two different directions and say, "Whatever is causing this now collapses and moves out of my energy field." Then say, "I don't see anything here." If necessary, allow the burning wands to move and take different positions during the visualization. Stay with the images as long as they have potency. You may repeat the command as often as you wish during these movements of the visualization.

If the problem persists, imagine you are sliding into an alternate reality, a new dimension where it doesn't exist, and state that I am now in an alternate reality where this problem doesn't exist. Go back to the first moment you remember feeling it in your reality. Live through that moment without the problem appearing. See the scene through to the end as it would have played out without the problem. How would you have felt the next morning when you woke up? What have you learned? Write it down.

Restarting Your Software

Here you imagine your holographic body and universe shut down. Visualize total darkness. Then imagine the switch being turned and the software is on again, just like a computer goes from dark to light when turned on. Feel the restart as light swirling and moving through your holographic body. Something has changed. Look for what it is. You are not the same. Something was eliminated and cleared in the reboot. Daily reboots enable your life to transform at a maximum pace.

Restore Points

In your mind, go back to a time before the ailment appeared, when you remember feeling extremely well.

Declare, I set this as a restore point, and give a name to that moment, if not a date and time.

To access a resource state for manifesting, go to the moment before you manifested one of your greatest wishes. Give the experience a name and an approximate date and write it down. Then find another moment when you manifested a deep wish. Again name it, date it and write it down. Repeat this process until you can't think of anymore greatest wishes fulfilled. Here are some examples from my clients:

"Manifesting my true mate in June 1996. Manifestation was instantaneous—I literally looked out the window and saw 'him.'"

"That day at work in 2004 when I was distraught about my job and suddenly received a phone call with a great new job offer."

"That day in April or May when I received part of an inheritance that instantly cleared my credit card balances."

"That day in 2010 when I received a settlement that solved my financial problems."

"That day in July 2007 when I found the perfect home in my dream location."

Now suppose that somehow your negative emotions are activated at work and you feel disinclined to continue working. Resistance sets in, as so often happens. How do you get back on track?

Start by remembering the truth, as the truth always sets you free, in this case free of negative emotions. What is truth? You are inside a 'story' run by the equivalent of a computer software program. Negative emotional responses are built into the default emotions part of the program. You simply accessed a default emotional pattern from the program in response to an event.

Let's say the default is anger, which quickly rose up within you shifting your peaceful and creative energy in a direction that you believe does not support the kind of work you wish to do. Your concern is not only for the discomfort of the anger, but for its interruption of the positive emotions you believe you need to complete your task. You fear that the negative vibration will attract wrong action and you want to act rightly. The problem therefore isn't the anger per se, but your fear of what it means for the work you are about to perform.

Your emotional state is often your personal albatross. When it's good, you feel good as you work. When it's bad, you feel discomfort while you work. Consider the possibility that the work is impervious to these shifts in your emotional state and that your emotional state has been designed and customized by the program not to interfere. Because it is impossible for you to work in a vacuum and avoid human contact and human irritations, all that is required then is your attention and your body engaged with the task.

If you recognize that your emotions are irrelevant to the task, whether good or bad as you would label it, then it doesn't matter what happens with that difficult person and what effect that brief interaction has on your energy system.

Say to yourself: Even though I feel this anger at B. for his tone, and further believe that this anger can prevent me from being in the vibration I need to be in, in order to do the highest quality of work, I now realize that nothing can interfere with my work. My work has been custom designed to transcend my petty emotions as they shift day by day and minute by minute. As long as I am physically able to work, which I am and shall continue to be, I can do so faultlessly and flawlessly. The only difference in the experience is my subjective mood. If I am happy, the work is more enjoyable, it feels better and I can easily believe in and accept its high quality. If I am unhappy, it is simply work that I perform and more difficult to feel good about in that moment. But the crucial factor is that, either way, I can do my work effectively and need not fear the results.

Chapter 12

Oneness and Love

How do you feel the oneness with your greater self, the god of you? Try the following exercise: Close your eyes. Sense your body; notice its outlines. Feel the air around you touching and surrounding your body, as if hugging it from all angles. Now see yourself as a figure surrounded by air. Visualize the air surrounding you as a teaming soup of lightwaves. Experience yourself as immersed in these lightwaves, these lightwaves coursing through you, but somehow you retain the outline of a form.

Open your eyes.

This soup of light is the consciousness of God, your greater self. This light coursing through you is the consciousness of God as you, being you. This outline of a human form is an illusion, but it enables you to maintain identity in this experience.

The image of you in a soup of lightwaves, a world of lightwaves, is closest to the reality of your situation. There are no solid floors or ceilings or walls; there is no actual three dimensional body. It is simply coded lightwaves.

Coded lightwaves are the way in which the program specifies what something appears to be. None of this exists outside the mind of God. The mind of God is the program, the consciousness of God is the waves of light encoded with information about how light is to appear and function. These are detailed codes that if further deconstructed can be understood to be simply bundled thoughts in the mind of God.

What is the Cross? Unrelated to the Christian symbol, the Cross is the perception of lightwaves moving from right to left or left to right as well as from up to down or down to up. A problem in the physical illusion body is perceived when the movement of lightwaves is somehow blocked.

There are many defaults in the program that allow lightwave movement to appear to be blocked in order to create the various ills that are designed for a given Life-Time experience in the physical illusion. An ailment is then held in perception by the intersection of the Cross.

This intersection is in the exact middle of both poles of energy, not higher on one pole, as it is in the Christian symbol.

As you sense into a problem area of your physical body, ask yourself how are you not perceiving the movement of the Cross. What would the movement of the Cross energies feel like or look like in your mind's eye if they were moving freely? You can restore correct and full flow of the Cross by imagining holding a small cross of bright gold light and then placing it over the problem area. Place it into the problem area. Sometimes not one, but many Crosses are needed, completely surrounding the area. If in your mind's eye a funnel is created surrounded by Crosses, and an opening seems to appear in which an arm reaches in and seems to be moving around inside you, feeling for something and then grasps an object, allow all this to take place and for the arm to grasp the object and remove it from your illusion body. Let the body speak. Take pen and paper and write down what it says. It might go like this.

"I am your chronic illusion pain or discomfort and constant illusion energy movement in your left shoulder blade area. I am the problem that won't go away and leave you in peace. My constant presence distracts you in everything you do. You fear me, because you are drawn to me with a kind of fascination, a kind of compulsiveness, as if you must attend to me, must work on me, must get rid of me, must heal me in order for you to have peace in your body and be able to focus on other things. I am otherwise known as the Monkey on Your Back. I manage to pull your attention to me whenever you work with energy or work on yourself spiritually. I often pull your attention when you work in the physical illusion, or simply are present to the physical illusion. I inspire you to try out all kinds of healing methodologies on me, and you try this and that, sometimes with momentary effect, but nothing seems to permanently free you of what you perceive to be an imbalance in your energy flow, or tension in your left shoulder. You then write off all these methods as worthless and wonder what the answer is. You have sought all kinds of answers as to what is causing this discomfort and applied all kinds of solutions, but nothing alters whatsoever in your physical perception. Yet you have never tried talking to me to find out what I am and why I am here."

Who are you and why are you here?

"I am the part of you that is being ignored and denied. This part of you desires to have the experience of deep and profound love and oneness with others while in the physical illusion experience. I am here to restore you to love."

How do you accomplish that?

"I cause you to seek, to remain dissatisfied with what-is and to remember that there is an unresolved matter, the matter of love. It can only be healed when you learn to love in a way that has until now eluded you completely. The highest purpose of your lifetime is to learn about this love, to apply this learning to your teachings and to help others return to love. In the return to love is the solution to all the ills that beset you in the physical illusion. This love encompasses all that is; this love is the All that Is. All That Is, dear one, is Love. But what this love really looks like, how it operates and what it appears to be in action in the physical illusion is so far removed from common concepts of love, it is a revelation of truth that has until now never been expressed in your illusion world. You are being called to become a spigot of love, with a teaching so desperately needed by the others in your illusion, yourself included, it will dramatically heal not only the physical, but the financial, the social, the emotional and the mental. You are being called to love.

First is the matter of peace. Peace is a vibrational frequency on one level; it is a perceptual state on another; it is an affect on another; and it is a gift on another. Peace is the prize above all others. Peace is the number one purpose of a call to love. Love presages peace, one cannot exist without the other, but love comes first.

This is little known - Love presages peace. The two are not interchangeable, their order not reversible. Love is the state which must be achieved before there can be peace. Peace automatically follows love. Therefore, the goal is love, not peace. Love is peace in action.

It is believed that love is a feeling in the heart, or for some, in the loins, it is the welling up of affection for something cherished and adorable, it is the longing for the missing loved one, it is the desire to do good or to help someone. But love is none of these things. It is not a feeling, it is not doing good for a loved one, it is not sex, passion, lust, or any of the emotions associated with sex and sexual attraction., it is not the chemical reaction that seems to afflict those who have 'fallen in love.' It is not even present among most of those who marry, on the day of their public union.

If love is not doing good, is not caring for your loved ones, is not feelings of affection, is not passion and desire, then what is love? Love is the absence of all motive, the motive to do good and the motive to do anything at all. Love is no thing, it is no feeling. Love is objective consciousness. It is the ability to think with the mind of God, to actually hold this as your desire and intent, and the ability to view things shorn of their cultural underpinnings and conditioned responses.

Love is the mind of God pure and simple. This is how the phrase, God is Love came about. God is consciousness, unconditioned consciousness, objective consciousness.

Love is a state of consciousness. So what, you ask, are the feelings of desire in your heart to help heal a wounded soul or to give to loved ones? That is the love which comes with the default program. The default comes with a whole host of feelings and emotions, preprogrammed into the story. These emotions are activated, those buttons pressed so to speak, when your greater self wants to steer you in certain directions. Thus, the feelings of love and inspiration and motivation that are felt in your heart, and perhaps accompanied by an idea of how you might express them, come from the default software and are part of your storyline.

That pain in your shoulder which we have advised that you need to transform in love is actually a diversion of light from your fifth, sixth and seventh chakras or energy centers. It is a shunt of sorts that awaits your awakening to Objective Consciousness. When you have reached a certain stage of your awareness of truth, and demonstrating sufficient willingness to act on your instructions, the energy that is being shunted to the left will flow into new corridors, some of it dissolving into the nothingness from which it came, and other of it stimulating higher centers of what you perceive to be your brain but is actually the seat of your Objective Consciousness. So stop trying to heal it, as you are wasting time focusing on something that is not an actual physical matter, not even in terms of the illusion. It is a matter of readiness. You are readying for a new state of consciousness, one that far expands you beyond where you have lived most of your life, even in the decades since your first major expansion. So realize that what is in your shoulder is simply Objective Consciousness, the consciousness of God or Love that awaits its restoration to its Seat of Power within your consciousness, its seat of primacy. It is nothing to fear, although we understand that you perceive it as a discomfort. And your medical helpers might diagnosis it in this way or that. Ignore all diagnoses. Seek to restore yourself to Love, the Objective Consciousness of God, and the discomfort will fade as if a distant memory.

Because Objective Consciousness is so different from your everyday consciousness, it must be grown into through many stages. Each book you write and complete in this series represents a stage of consciousness that you and your readers achieve just by being present to the material and completing the exercises. As you move through this and the books that are to come, your consciousness continues to expand until one day you have reached a state of Objective Consciousness sufficient to recalibrate your entire illusion experience."

Chapter 13

FORMATTING YOUR DISC

Let us address formatting your disc. Yes, dear one, you now receive a new game of life, a game that in the playing brings joy, expansion, happiness, grandeur and blessings to your life. Any player will receive these benefits, as translated by their greater self for the purposes of their Life-time experience.

This game does not demand that a story character try to enhance themself by making certain declarations. This game does not require turning away from the illusion world of limitation, does not require denying it, or playing an opposite game of reclaiming power.

When you believe you need to reclaim power you give power to the illusion limitations that are exactly what they sound like: illusions. The world in which your body moves, thinks and lives is like a computer program. It is designed to make you feel that you are struggling against odds at all times, and always in a position of needing to do, have, acquire, or be more than you currently appear to be. This is known as the game of limitation.

The degree of detail in this software that provides endless aspects of limitation is profound, almost inconceivable. The default program for most players involves an entire life lived in relation to limitation, whether the overcoming of illusion limitations or the succumbing to illusion limitations. The story is determined ahead of time. The only factor that can influence the story is the degree to which any given player is programmed in advance to awaken to their true self in the story.

Players are programmed to varying degrees with the ability to see that they are the 'ghost in the machine.' Some stories are simply about living the default life, which is a life lived in relation to limitation. Other stories allow more degrees of freedom. If you are interested in these teachings or are the one writing them, you have been given more degrees of freedom, many more than the vast majority of players in the illusion.

These teachings will gradually lead you out of the maze of limitation. They are the bread crumbs dropped in the woods that allow Hansel and Gretel to find their way home. All you need to do is read these teachings and apply the exercises. If you do not perform the exercises you will not receive the benefit, no matter how many times you read these teachings.

How to format your disc: in preparation for the Choose and Receive It game, you must first access a disc, format it, and activate it; then begins your daily command procedures.

Access a Disc

By this we mean create an etheric disc, one that arises in your imagination. Think of it as a CD or DVD containing the consciousness of someone who represents maximum degrees of freedom, someone who seems to have the ability to create anything they want. This person can be someone you know, someone you admire in your life, or someone from history within the illusion. It can also be an imaginary character, such as an archetypal or religious being, i.e., a superhero from comic books or a religious leader.

For the purposes of this game, select someone synonymous with the power to create. Who maximally embodies the power to create? In so choosing, please know that if you are dissatisfied with this choice later on, for any reason, you may reformat your disc and choose again.

Imagine that this person or being is reaching inside their mind or their heart, removing a dazzling gold disc and slipping it into an imaginary 'slot' somewhere in your illusion body. That slot is the DVD player, so to speak. We recommend that you choose to imagine your greater self is the source of this disc and is providing this disc.

You may conceive of your greater self as a large egg-shaped consciousness of dazzling white light with a cord of its awareness extended into the top of your head and down through the center of your entire illusion body. The disc is then seen to travel down this cord and into a slot at the top of your head, or further down, into your heart. Imagine a pulse of white light surging from your greater self down the cord into the disc, further charging this disc with power.

Your own greater self is the best choice because it is the creator of all that you know to be your reality, and therefore, is the creative force of your personal universe. By downloading the disc, you now have received your greater self's power to create. It has been provided to you in the story. It was always your power, but seemed inaccessible until now. You may rejoice, for you now have accessed the disc that enables you to create from within the story. What remains is to format the disc and activate the disc.

Format the Disc

To format the disc that is now installed in your illusion body you make the following declarations:

I am the creator of my reality.

I take responsibility for my creations.

I choose with full consciousness of my choices.

My choices bring untold benefit to everyone involved.

My choices support the highest and best in every situation.

My choices instantly outmanifest in my illusion world.

As you make these declarations, imagine the disc spinning as fast as possible, and shining as brightly as possible. Watch and see if the colors change. How do they change? Spin it so fast, it's just a whir. Watch and see if the disc changes shape or placement. Follow the spinning disc in your mind's eye and let it do what it will do.

Activate the Disc

To activate the disc, imagine it spinning like a top somewhere inside your illusion body. Imagine the color shifting from gold to white to a white light as bright as you can possibly envision. Get your clue from bolts of lightning you have seen in the sky, that kind of electric white. Imagine the disc crackling and snapping like electricity. If it turns into a blue-white light, that is good. Now in your mind's eye, watch it spinning, watch it growing in size. When it appears to grow to a size that encompasses your entire illusion body, you have activated the disc. You will feel yourself embraced in the spinning disc, and then it will suddenly stop.

The disc will be your power tool for coding the lightwaves of your illusion to bring forth your choices as commanded by you. Next, we will discuss how to correctly make your choices and how to command them into being.

Chapter 14

The Art and Science of Making Choices

Dear reader, first of all I thank you for coming back to the work, as it awaits you with great eagerness and joy. Yes, the work is alive. It is alive in consciousness and wishes to be brought to life in your illusion reality.

In this chapter you are going to be taught how to create illusions while installed inside an illusion world and an illusion body. The mystery of creation will become crystal clear. The alteration of illusions that limit your scope of freedom and self expression is now possible. Prepare yourself for rapid change, as the shift is instantaneous once all of the steps have been completed. By this I mean, once you have accessed, formatted and activated your disc, then chosen what you wish to receive correctly and commanded it into your illusion in the way I instruct, that which you have selected to receive or experience must occur.

To begin, choose one thing you wish to occur right now, one thing you are ready to receive in this moment if it were for example to fall into your lap. Select the one thing that is most important to you at this time, making sure that you are completely ready for that thing to happen right now. An example of lack of readiness for that 'thing' to happen right now is as follows: you desire a new love partner, however, you are not at the moment showered, dressed and in the condition which you would normally be in if you were trying to attract a new love partner. Or, you are working against deadline with no real time or focus available for a love partner. In these instances, do not command a love partner into your illusion. Wait for the moment when you are available and prepared to meet that love partner.

Again, to choose one must choose correctly. It may seem silly to never ask for that which you are unready in this very moment to receive, but that, dear one, is the essence of correct choice. You will always succeed in creating illusions if you demonstrate total readiness in the moment for the illusion you are seeking to create.

Step 1: Determine the area of life in which you wish to receive change and which, if it were to happen, you are physically, emotionally and mentally ready in this very moment to receive: Choose from one of these areas: love, marriage, home, family, career, job, health, creativity, success, money, education, friends.

Then write: I choose (select the area in which you wish to create a new illusion.)

For purposes of this exercise, let us say you choose money. Now write out a description of the way money currently appears in your reality. In other words, describe the problem or situation you wish to re-create, but state it in the past tense. Always describe it in terms where you acknowledge that you have created each part of it as in the following examples from my clients:

I have created Money appearing to not flow into my life for the past six months.

I have created the illusion of credit card debt.

I have created the illusion of needing money from my partner and my partner resenting giving it to me.

I have created the illusion of not having money for a new car even though my car is 10 years old.

I have created the illusion of not having money for health insurance and dental insurance.

I have created the illusion of not having money to live in a quiet, peaceful home of my own.

I have created the illusion that I am not able to 'make money.'

I have created the illusion of feeling deep upset and pain over my lack of money and feeling like my life wasn't worth living and that God was against me or didn't care about me at all.

Now define exactly what you wish to create in the area of money. State it in the present tense as if it has already occurred. Here are some examples from my clients:

I now create an abundance of money flowing into my illusion for my personal use in the amount of at least $10,000 per month.

I now create having zero balances on my monthly credit card statements.

I now create financial independence from my husband.

I now create having more than enough money to buy or lease a brand new car.

I now create having more than enough money to have excellent health and dental insurance.

I now create having more than enough money to buy my own home and live in the environment of my choice.

I now create having more than enough money for every constructive wish, want, need, and desire that I have.

I now create having an extraordinary ability to "make money" in six figure quantities or more.

I now create feeling ecstatic, joyful, powerful, utterly relieved and unbelievably grateful for receiving large quantities of money.

At this point you should be pleased that you have completed the first presentation of your situation and your recreated illusion. Let us take a moment here to understand the meaning of recreating your illusion.

The world you inhabit is a concept in the mind of your greater self. It operates like computer software, replete with a program with default settings and, to varying degrees, the potential for customization. Your personal reality is specifically designed by your greater self to take place in a certain context and to achieve a certain purpose according to the needs of your greater self in its unending exploration of consciousness. The customization of your software can only be achieved within certain boundaries set by your greater self. In other words, if it has determined you will be a figure skater, you cannot simply skip off and become a physicist. Nor would you choose to, as your interests and choices are always in natural alignment with the program. If you are choosing to change some aspect of the program, you must know that this change is desired by your greater self and is allowed by your greater self. You would not want to make this change if your greater self did not want you to make it.

That said, there are many desires that reflect default cultural programs and do not represent the true desires of your greater self (i.e., the specific desires of your greater self for your story). For each desire you wish to create, you must consult your greater self for its approval of this desire and you must determine exactly what your greater self has permitted for you in this arena. For example, you might want the power and influence of a billionaire, but your greater self has not determined that experience as an essential part of your story. As a matter of fact, your story might entail a modest income in a service occupation such as teaching in the public schools. Your hunger for wealth and power would in this case be a default cultural program and not a true desire. Therefore, your program would not be customizable for this choice.

Before you issue your commands based on the choices you made regarding, in this case, money, you must determine if these commands are within the potential for customization for your program. In other words, is it the plan of your greater self for you to experience the wealth and success you are choosing? Or, you might ask, what is the plan of my greater self for my financial well-being? It is essential to seek input from your own greater consciousness before attempting to alter the program.

Receiving the correct answer from your higher consciousness is critical in forming your command. When you make your command, it must be in full alignment with the plan of your greater self for your illusion story. If your command is not in alignment, it will not manifest, pure and simple.

Commands in full alignment with your greater self manifest rapidly, and in some cases instantaneously. Your job is to ascertain the intention of your greater self in the matter of money as it pertains to your story.

How do you access your greater self? The author of this work is accessing their greater self with every word they write. It is I, the greater self of the author, who writes these words, not the story character. However, the author has aligned with me and allowed the book to be written through them, so to speak. They have agreed to take on this task to completion, even if they do not fully understand or approve of its content. This is true alignment—a suspension of judgment and a leap of faith. Every act of alignment with your greater self involves a suspension of judgment and a leap of faith.

The suspension of judgment is needed to allow your greater self to express its plan without your editing or eliminating any facet of the plan, even if it does not match your desires. The leap of faith is your trust that the greater you is the part of you that has infinite knowledge and infinite truth and is, in fact, the master of your destiny. It may appear there are two, you and It, but in fact there is only one. When you access your greater you, you rise above the default cultural and personal programs of the story-you and discern the true intent of the greater you as it explores consciousness through your story.

From a state of consciousness in alignment with your greater self, now ask—what is your plan for, or what should I know about, my financial well-being? What is the potential for customization of my program in the area of money?

Now meditate on these two questions and imagine a voice in your head answering you. Write down what the voice says. Here is an example, paraphrased from one of my clients:

Beloved, you have full freedom to maximize your income. There are no limits in your program when it comes to your personal income. You have been designed to seek what you love—knowledge, freedom, and truth. The lover of money is designed to seek only more and more money. Within your total persona lies certain limits to your focus on making money. Therefore, you are not designed to be an individual whose claim to fame is their massive wealth.

You are designed to prosper through the avenues that you naturally pursue for your self-expression and professional growth. Do not fear your money circumstance. It is designed to turn around with a rapidity and suddenness that will astound you. You will be restored to a degree of financial well being that will allow for everything you have listed in your choices list and much, much more. You will be well-compensated for your work and will see a relationship between what you have invested and what you receive. You will be successful in your field.

There are many more productive and successful and abundant years left in your life timeline, therefore you can be encouraged and comforted to know that you are already abundant and have zero balances on your credit cards. It just has not caught up to your illusion yet. When you make your command, make it knowing that we support you fully in your abundant life.

Chapter 15

THE ART OF COMMAND

In this section, you will take the information given to you by your greater self and you will fashion a command that integrates the input from your greater self with your choice of money. Here you must specify for your own clarification what your greater self decrees for your degrees of customization in this arena and how this decree will be reflected in your command.

Let us say that your greater self indicates that you will be abundantly compensated for your teaching abilities and that your financial situation will flip rapidly and suddenly into financial abundance. It is incumbent on you as the creator from within your illusion, in alignment with your greater self's design for your illusion story, to command exactly when, how, and in what financial quantity this turnaround will take place.

Write your command down in the present tense.

Make it one sentence, as short and to the point and specific as possible. Give a date, a time, an amount, how you feel and what you are doing. Here is an example from one of my clients.

I command that my financial situation turns around with such power, rapidity and suddenness, I am stunned. It is (state date) and I am at my desk when I receive a phone call from a company offering me a new account.

Now ask your greater self—will you create this illusion by (state date)? If yes, then make the command verbally in the full power and presence of God, the creator. If no, then ask your greater self what the acceptable time frame is, and/or whether this illusion needs to be modified in any way.

In this case, the answer is no. Your finances will turn around suddenly and dramatically, but not that day. "Then when?" you ask. (State new date) is your answer. So now your command is as follows:

I command that on (state new date), I am in my office at my desk with the clock reading 3 p.m. and I am holding in my hand and looking with joy at a check written out to me in the amount of $10,000 or more. This is a down payment for my work on my new account to be delivered by (state date), in an excellent deal with an ethical company that is guaranteed to pay me at least

$100,000 over the coming year. Let this be done. Let this be so. Thank you for this or something much, much better.

Now you have your command. Is it showing the desired date, time, place, what exactly you are doing and what is happening? Good. Now you must install the command in your disc. This will enable the command to go to work instantly to recreate your illusion story such that it naturally leads to your receiving that check and having that deal by the specified date.

Installation of Your Command

Bring up the image of your disc as a bright gold CD or DVD located in the region of your brain or heart. See it start to spin like a top. When it is spinning so fast it is a complete blur, slowly and loudly declare your command. You may read your command, imagining that the words are being absorbed by the disc, copied by the disc, so to speak. You can do this by imagining the words floating through the air and entering the spinning disc. After each phrase, allow it to enter the disc, then, in your imagination, hear the phrase repeated by the disc. Make sure that the words you hear are clear. If necessary, have the disc repeat a word that is not clear. Do this now.

Example: State your command out loud in short phrases

'I command that on (state date)'

See the words floating into the disc

Hear the disc repeat the words like a tape recorder:

'I command that on (state date)'

Make sure the words you hear are said clearly, especially dates, times, and amounts.

If, for example the date is not heard clearly, have the disc repeat it until you hear it stated clearly.

'(State date)'

Then continue with the next phrase in your command and proceed in this fashion until the entire command has been stated aloud, absorbed by the disc and repeated back to you by the disc clearly.

Congratulations. You have now installed your command. The first time is always the most challenging. Choosing your commands correctly and installing them on your disc will take just a few short minutes of your day as you become comfortable with this process over time.

Your disc now contains your command and must create the reality you have commanded. All you need to do is ask your greater self: what, if anything, do I need to be, do or have to be fully in alignment with this command? Listen for the answer. Write it down. Ask your greater self for clarification if need be, then do what you have been instructed to do to the best of your ability.

If you have chosen correctly and are in true alignment with this command, it is unlikely that you will be asked to do anything further in that moment. But if you are, there should be a sense of ease on your part in acquiescing to your instructions. If you feel resistance to any part of the instructions, engage in a dialogue with your greater self, always writing down your questions and its answers. Ask your greater self how to come into alignment with its request. If, after following this process, you notice that you have not taken the necessary actions for alignment, it is time to go back to the beginning and review every step in this process.

Choosing your command is the most critical part of the entire creation process.

Checklist:

Choose the area you wish to create in.

Ask your greater self what is the degree of customization available to you here.

Make a command.

Install the command.

Ask your greater self whether there is anything further you need to be, do or have to align with this command.

Carry out the alignment instructions.

If resistance arises, question your greater self as to how to overcome this resistance.

If resistance persists, there has been a flaw in the command process. Return to Choices, the first part of the process, and begin the entire process again.

Daily Commands

The command process is available to you every day. We suggest making no more than one new command per day. Not each command need be for a major change. Small shifts are highly desirable daily commands.

For example:

You may command changes in your emotional reaction to something that you previously resisted.

You may command changes in your experience that represent one small step closer to a goal.

You may command changes in your presentation of self when in the presence of certain others.

You may command subtle feeling shifts that increase joy.

You may command feeling better in a specific area.

You may command performing better in a specific area.

You may command perceptual changes—seeing something in a different light that changes your point of view totally.

You may command happiness to be present even in the difficult moments of your day.

Every command is installed in your disc. When commands are meant to shift your emotions, behaviors, or perceptions in the desired direction on an ongoing basis, this should be stated in the command.

Some commands only address a single situation and others are intended to alter emotions, behavior, and perception in a continuous fashion. Always be specific when designing your command. A good phrase to add for an emotion, behavior or perception that you wish to be changed perpetually is:

This feeling of/action of/perception of ________ continues, increases and expands on a daily basis. An example would be: This feeling of joy continues, increases and expands on a daily basis.

If you want to cause a permanent decrease or cessation of a problematic feeling, action or perception, be sure to phrase it in a positive way. Never state a problem in your command; only state the desired outcome, feeling, action or perception.

An example for ending your procrastination of homework assignments would be: With every passing day, I find it easier and easier to get my homework done on time.

An example for ending irritation with your child's behavior would be: I feel a sense of peace and understanding when interacting with Ashley, and this peace and understanding continues, increases and expands on a daily basis.

Analysis of A Failed Command

When attempting to use commands to manifest, it may take a bit of analysis to understand why your command may have failed. Let us look closely at a failed attempt to manifest a command using this system. This case study is from one of my students who is a screenwriter.

I command that on (state date), I am in my office at my desk with the clock reading 3 p.m. and I am holding in my hand and looking with joy at a check written out to me in the amount of at least $100,000.00. This is a down payment for my book and script, plus two additional spec scripts to be delivered by (state date) and (state date) respectively, in an excellent deal with ethical buyers that is guaranteed to pay me at least $3,000,000.00 (three million dollars) over the next two years. Let this be done. Let this be so. Thank you for this or something much, much better.

In the screenwriter's storyline, it is now weeks later and this command did not manifest. Let us review what took place. After he made his command, he became aware of an upcoming presentation on book to film projects and knew he should attend. There he met Ben Adams (not his real name), a Hollywood agent for book to film projects, made the necessary contact with him and engaged his interest in the project. Adams requested that the writer send him the book and script. Everything appeared to proceed according to the command up to this point. This indicates that the command was in alignment with the screenwriter's greater self.

However, as the weeks passed, this party did not respond to the screenwriter's request for a status update. The fulfillment date for his command came and went without a ripple. On the surface, this represents a failure of the system, but let us look more closely at what occurred.

The screenwriter wondered whether Ben Adams was right for the project. But after some discussion, we were better able to understand what transpired. Who is Ben Adams? He is a creation of consciousness, playing a part in a virtual story. Even while seeking his help in selling his project, the screenwriter felt a subtle revulsion. Every time he thought of him he felt this revulsion, this dislike lurking beneath the surface desire for him to become his agent. The writer ignored this feeling because he believed that he must accept working with people who he doesn't like in order to achieve his goals, as if he has no say over who he works with, but must take whoever shows up.

This feeling of dislike—who created that? The writer's greater self created those negative feelings to signal that Ben Adams was not suitable for his project.

This was purely a learning experience for this writer. He needed to learn this lesson about liking the people he works with, about his right to command that the people he works with on his projects are people he likes and respects.

This experience revealed what was missing from this command—the part about working with people at every stage who you like and respect and who like and respect you. You can go even further and command people of enormous affinity and like mind who you truly enjoy and love to come aboard for your project. Doesn't that feel great?

So you see the flaw in this command. The lack of results offered a lesson; you are learning how to process your results in manifesting reality. This learning is the most important part of this entire process of reality creation, as it will help you tune up your command for the repeat installation. In this way, any command that does not occur as ordered may be reconstituted and reinstalled with different results. You fine tune the process and you fine tune the results as well.

Exciting, isn't it? Now your attitude toward this little misadventure has shifted, has it not, dear one? It doesn't look like a failure anymore; instead you may view yourself as a scientific experimenter in manifesting reality. When the result does not appear, look always to the command. An investigation of the command, the events that followed, your honest feelings and thoughts, your degree of alignment, etc., will bring forth new information that will enable you to release a blockage and issue a command likely to produce a far more pleasing result.

Now the screenwriter knows that he wishes to work with people he feels greatly attuned with and who he loves.

You are the commander, the creator, and you can have it any way you choose. Why choose to be a desperado who will take anyone that comes along? For many, that has been your unspoken approach up to now, which has sunk your ship over and over again. Why? Because you really don't want to work with people you don't like or don't respect. In this case, the writer didn't believe he actually had a choice in the matter when it came to ordering the sale of a Hollywood project. Now you know that you can choose the type of people who participate in your projects because you are the Commander in Chief of your world.

This same attitude of 'taking what comes along' has likely permeated your entire life, particularly in your choice of lovers, friends and jobs. You did not determine ahead of time all that you refuse to accept and all that you truly desired in lovers, friends and jobs, thus allowing your life to be overtaken by disharmonious situations. You did not determine this because you did not believe you could have the lovers, friends and jobs you truly desired. You also needed to experience many of these situations in order to learn what it is you truly wanted. But, in truth, dear one, you learned what you needed to know a long time ago, yet continued to choose inharmonious situations because you believed you could not have what you really want.

Finally, we have reached a milestone where you and your greater self can unite in creating that which you really want, unhampered by the belief that you cannot have what you really want. That belief has made the Commander in Chief careless in designing commands. What is left out is a critical missing part of the design, which then causes you to unconsciously reject the people, places and things you are engaging with.

The outer result appears to be your failure or loss, but in fact, you rejected the person, place or thing which lacked the full design your heart desired.

So in reviewing the incident with Ben Adams, you may now understand that the screenwriter did not like this agent but believed that he must accept whoever comes along if it means the success of his project, all the while unconsciously rejecting him. This experience occurred to demonstrate the importance of recognizing everything you want in a situation, including good feelings about the people involved and the experience of their strong appreciation, recognition and respect for you. Now, does that mean that the screenwriter should have refused to engage with this agent or to send him his material? No. The agent was there for a reason—to help him clarify this issue.

Going forward, you have learned that you must insert into your command the feelings you want to have in the relationship or situation, and expect that you will get them. Now let us proceed to reformulate this command:

I command that on (state date), I am in my office at my desk with the clock reading 3 p.m. and I am holding in my hand and looking with joy at a check written out to me in the amount of at least $100,000.00. This is a down payment for my book and script, in a three script deal that includes two additional blind spec scripts to be delivered by (state date) and (state date) respectively. This is a profitable deal for me with ethical buyers whom I really like and feel appreciated by, and is guaranteed to pay me at least $3,000,000.00 (three million dollars) over the next two years. Let this be done. Let this be so. Thank you for this or something much, much better.

I then advised the screenwriter to issue a command for the type of person who will represent him in this deal, such as an agent or manager.

I command that a powerful agent or manager, who I love and trust completely and who loves, appreciates, recognizes and respects me, now appears in my life to represent me in the script deal. This agent or manager is a brilliant negotiator who knows how to get the best deal for their clients, and they smoothly negotiate a better deal than I ever imagined possible that protects all my interests and maximizes my reputation, profits and current and future earnings in the industry

.

Chapter 16

A Diver of Pearls

Dear reader, there is nothing wrong with being interested in what mirrors (those mirroring your cultural programs) have to say about creation and the nature of reality. Realize that whatever you are called to read has something there for you. Perhaps it will stimulate an idea that enhances your work or your life. Your greater self communicates with you in many ways. The more excited you are about life, about creation and about manifesting, the more energized your study of this work will be.

You are the product of a greater self that lives through you and uses your eyes as the window into your reality. Do you really think that the greater you, the all powerful creator of you, judges the story-you? Absolutely not. It makes no sense. The story-you is exploring all facets of the storyline set into motion by the greater you for purposes of expanding the consciousness of the greater you in certain arenas.

Each Life-Time journey answers questions for the greater you and is viewed as valuable and invaluable. There is never judgment, ridicule, criticism, disparaging, or any other denigration of the story-you in the mind or heart of the greater you. The greater you and the story-you are one and the same, with the story-you living out directly a storyline that allows the greater you to answer questions and raise others.

There is never an end to the explorations of consciousness carried on by the greater you, as expansion is its primary objective. The greater you is an Infinite Intelligence that continues to expand beyond all space and time, beyond reason, beyond words, beyond thoughts, beyond all forms of expression. It is an Infinite Expansion carried out by the story characters it creates to run the storylines.

The storyline you now run has an important, incomparable purpose and meaning for the greater you. Whether or not you value your story, the story has value for the greater you, as do you, its eyes and ears, its arms and legs. You are the warrior of light, the symbolic presence of your greater self in the story. As such, you really are your greater self and have a value far beyond the apparent value of a story character.

As the symbolic presence of your greater self you are destined to do great things and to live in a state of greatness. This greatness is available to you immediately once you understand your true nature as the symbolic presence of the Infinite within a limited story. The story always contains the Infinite, like the King in a chess game. He reigns over all other players and embodies the nobility and power of the Infinite. You are that nobility and power, you are that King. You are the symbolic presence of the Infinite within your story. Now live as such. Act from the Infinite depths of your being. Live from the expansive heights of your being, and express with the scope, power and destiny of the greater you.

You are not just a story character, a human being, a man or a woman. You are a mini-God, the homunculus of an Infinite Ever-Expanding Consciousness. As such, there is grandeur in every moment of your existence. Your gestures instigate the rippling of wavelengths far beyond the boundaries of your story. Your actions have meaning in every little detail for the whole of Existence. Live in the consciousness of your greatness and you will find that life jumps up to meet you in the place of greatness. If ever you felt little and insignificant, this will cure the self-diminishing thoughts that distract you from the truth. Never forget the truth of who you are.

You did not create your life, dear one. That is the first thing you need to know. The life you lead is and always has been created by the greater you.

Why would the greater you create such an incomplete, fragmented life, you might ask? You imagine that the greater you would create a great life, not this series of frustrating and unsatisfying relationships, jobs and circumstances.

However you feel about your storyline, the truth still remains like a rock, like a fortress. Feelings are passing shadows over timeless truth. It is the truth you need to orient toward, not feelings.

Whatever feelings you may have about your life and the way it has gone, the truth is that this is the life your greater self has chosen for you. You do not create from within the story until there has been a return to alignment with your greater self.

When your state of mind is critical of the way your life has gone and of the structure and content of your present, you are out of alignment with your greater self and lose the ability to create in oneness with the greater part of you.

The paradoxical truth about acceptance of what-is is that it is the only path to create what you want. But this acceptance cannot be feigned, nor can it be partial. When acceptance of what-is is total, your power is restored in that moment and you have the ability to know the true path carved out by the greater you. That is the path you truly desire in your heart of hearts, not the path dictated by 'feelings.'

The path the greater you designed from the beginning is the path you wish to traverse in the depths of your heart. That path contains the pearls your greater you sent you in to gather. It is the pearls that are the purpose of your story, dear one, not the outer successes or the recognition of others. Even where there is success and recognition, it is orchestrated by your greater self only so that you can extract the pearls from that experience.

Your greater self takes you where the pearls are for your particular story character. The greater self harvests those pearls for its own expansion and glory. You are the pearl diver. With understanding of your role, comes recognition of the true purpose of each moment in your storyline. It is never for the obvious reasons.

When unsure about your next steps or about your place in the story, ask your greater self, what is the pearl in this moment? What is the pearl in this experience? Listen for the answer. If it does not come in that moment, know it will come at the right time and in a way that you will recognize as the answer to your question.

Know this—the right question always receives an unmistakable right answer. Asking right questions ensures a right response. When you ask for the pearl, you are asking a right question and you will be given an answer.

To summarize: the outer details of your story, which you may or may not approve of, are created by the greater you so that you may extract the pearls you have been sent to gather for the greater you in its infinite exploration of consciousness and gathering of experience.

You serve a purpose for your greater self. You are the diver of pearls. You would not exist if you did not have a critical purpose in the exploration of your greater self's consciousness. This purpose may not be what you think. It may have nothing to do with conventional outer world pursuits that you have been programmed to associate with spiritual growth, such as helping others or succeeding at some task. It does have everything to do with the pearls of wisdom and experience gathered by carrying out these outer world pursuits, no matter their outcome or trajectory in the story.

You are being asked to detach from judgment of your storyline and are being shown the greater purpose of your storyline. The default program contains `default responses that are culturally defined. Your suffering is always a default response derived from the program. To realize this is to have an instant solution.

Recognize that suffering is because of what you are telling yourself based on your cultural programming. Remind yourself that your greater self never judges your actions in the story, that it creates the story, it determines your actions, and it is only and always seeking the pearls within the story.

You would never have an experience if there wasn't a pearl for your greater self. This isn't to say that you are a martyr for your greater self, but that the storyline has a high and noble purpose far beyond the way it appears to your story character and to mirrors (other people) in the story. By aligning with the greater purpose of your story, you align with the greater you and regain your power to create.

The power to create within the story is a facet of realignment with your greater self. All that you then create is what your greater self creates with or without your conscious participation. You do not take the story in directions your greater self would not wish it to go as you and the greater self are one and the same.

Becoming conscious and creating in the story, is simply becoming conscious of your greater self and creating the story it already created for you. When you understand what your greater self is seeking in the story, you are joyfully engaged in seeking what your greater self wants.

Consciousness is understanding what your greater self is seeking in your story and allowing it to be without conflict, without conditions, without judgment. You are then one with your greater self and you create with peace and harmony in the story. Nothing can shake your peace and harmony because you know this is what your greater self has sent you in to experience. You look for the pearls, not the outer conditions. The miracle is that when you align with your greater self in seeking the pearls, you receive an anointment of power and find circumstances reshaping harmoniously around you.

The storm is over and it was always the storm, the self-created controversy about what is happening and why it is happening, what has happened and why it has happened, that caused you to feel unloved and abandoned in a hellish world. Hell is arguing with the storyline created by your greater self. The argument creates negative emotions that blur your vision and block your sense of purpose.

When you feel separated from your greater self, you automatically descend into hell. Separation from your greater self occurs when you argue with the story it designed for you, when you agonize over the meaning of the story and the meaning of your life.

The temptation to argue with the story is best met with a command to your greater self to be shown the pearl. Affirming your awareness of the pearl and your greater self's purpose restores balance and vision. You may not have an immediate answer to your question, but you will receive an answer at the right time.

Just knowing that an answer must come to a right question brings peace and patience. Allow the story to unfold as it will, playing your part, asking the right questions, listening for the answers, and understanding always that the surface interpretation of the story is not wherein lies the pearl. You are the pearl diver and every moment of your story offers an opportunity to locate the pearls of your experience.

Chapter 17

THE MONOLITH OF CONSCIOUSNESS

You may ask, if the greater self is omniscient, then why does it need to seek anything? The answer is simple: the Consciousness of All That Is is ever-present everywhere, gathering knowledge by exploring experience. It is not a static Being, but an alive, expanding Intelligence.

The only purpose of consciousness is to continue exploring itself and thereby continuing to expand unto infinity. The exploration of consciousness permits the expansion of consciousness and that expansion has no beginning and no end. What else can an eternal infinite intelligence do, but continue to explore and expand itself?

That eternal infinite intelligence is the true you, expressing as the story character in the story line you now inhabit. That eternal infinite intelligence is also the story character of every storyline that has ever been and ever will be in every virtual world of its creation and in every sub-dimension of that virtual world.

Every virtual world has multiple dimensions and multiple alternate realities. The multiplicity of the Great One is so vast as to be uncountable and unfathomable by human minds. All the Great One does is create fields upon fields of experience that explore every facet of consciousness. The Great One has no ultimate purpose in its monolithic consciousness experiment, other than to know Itself in all of its infinitude, and to continue to expand itself throughout all of eternity.

The goal of consciousness is to create world upon world of exploration and innumerable mirrors or points of awareness from which to perceive these worlds of its own making. Existence is the soulful dance of a neverending, everlasting Mind.

The Caterpillar and the Butterfly

I am here to tell you that a solution to your problem arises, orchestrated by your greater self in the storyline of your life. It was always there awaiting the correct time and place. You cannot rush the schedule, and therefore I can only instruct that you remain calm and positive even while the old world shows up all around you with all of its discomforts and deprivations.

Have courage in the face of this transformation, which will be known by your acceptance of what-is and your fearlessness in the face of what will be. Act upon your internal compass. It is a flawless guide to your greater good—the path of your greater self in the story. Your only challenge is to release resistance to the conditions of your story as it now appears to be, and to open fully to the future, no matter what it may be. In that expansion lies your automatic transformation.

Be glad that the time for your automatic transformation to the next stage of your journey is nearly at hand. As you find the acceptance of what-is increasing and the fear of what will be decreasing, your train will move onto a new track and you will find yourself in a transformed reality with all new challenges and experiences. This is what your spirit longs for and what is on its way.

How much longer you ask? Is there anything you need to do in the story to facilitate this? Time is an illusion, dear one, but if you continue with this work, you will have your automatic transformation and will look back on these last days of your old life as the moments before the caterpillar burst from the cocoon.

Allow yourself to die to your current life, and keep an open mind about your new life. Is this a 'physical' death we are talking about, dear one? Know this, your exit from the story is no different than your automatic transformation to a different phase of the story. It doesn't matter what the next stage is. Fear of the future *is* fear of death and this is what must be overcome for the automatic transformation to take place both while in the story and while leaving the story.

No matter what your state of mind, dear one, in peace or strife, the story must and will change and you will make the transition to the next phase of your journey, So why not adopt an attitude of peace and acceptance, of calm and trust. It is all a journey, endless little deaths, and one final exit, yet none more or less meaningful than all the others, and none more or less painful or joyful than all the others.

Decide to transform with joy. Adopt the attitude of joy toward what awaits you, whether it is a transformation out of the physical story or a transformation within the physical story. It is all the same. Life and death are really one. To truly live, one must daily die to what-is. To die, one must daily live with what-is. I shall leave you to ponder those thoughts.

Chapter 18

LIVING WITH COURAGE

Automatic transformation is never preceded by complaints; it is preceded by acceptance of what-is, even a thorny and impossible what-is, as well as a fearlessness of what is to come even if what is to come is actual death—the end of the illusion—which is the ultimate transformation available within your story.

When troubles seem to press in all around, it is the time for courage, not fear and complaints. Live courageously, and your demons will be vanquished, slinking off into the shadows where they will be heard from no more. Live with courage. That is the theme for this chapter.

This life you lead is a storyline in a virtual world of your own creation, one of innumerable storylines that your Consciousness, the great All That Is, has run, continues to run and will always run for its own exploration, expansion, and amusement.

Are there themes to worlds, even virtual worlds, themes for eras in these virtual worlds? When you understand that your greater self engages in infinite exploration of all probable and improbable realities, you will realize that it is not unusual for your greater self to decide that a certain theme dominates a certain virtual reality playing field and that it gives a certain direction or slant to each person's story.

Each minute shift of direction or slant in a story results in a totally different story and totally different impressions for the consciousness running that story. Imagine how many varieties of experience can be had with the infinite thematic possibilities affecting virtual worlds and the personas that inhabit them.

You may be wondering what is the thematic slant of your virtual world. If you are reading this book, then the slant is reclaiming awareness of truth. That is what makes your virtual world special. It is one of the few with the story potential for reclaiming awareness of your true identity. Because this is available to all personas entering this frequency, a degree of awareness is present on a larger scale. But as we mentioned earlier, each story character is assigned as it were a bandwidth of consciousness sufficient to their story. For some the bandwidth is of a higher frequency than others, and the potential exists to access realms of truth usually unavailable in a virtual reality.

You, the faithful reader, are reading this book because you have an enhanced bandwidth with the potential for higher consciousness, for greater understanding of ultimate truth. Even so, the degrees of bandwidth are infinitesimal, leaving the achievement of full consciousness up to the greater you who designed your individual story.

In many of these cases, reaching full consciousness is consonant with exit from the story. In other stories, the character remains to experience their story from the enhanced perspective and, possibly, to assist those desiring to expand into higher ranges of their bandwidth.

The true you, the greater you, does not judge the actions of its story character. Remember, dear reader, the story character and the greater self are one and the same. Everything the greater self desires to experience through a story character in any given storyline must and will transpire.

The greater self typically runs multiple stories in multiple virtual worlds simultaneously. It creates the worlds and lives the stories across infinite virtual eras and in infinite virtual dimensions. That is how vast and grand your greater self is, yet this only describes a tiny percentage of your full capabilities.

If the truth is that you are one with Source, that only Source exists and that you are not the doer, then your job is to align with Source and allow it to move through you unhindered. When you are fully aligned, your reality resembles the life of your dreams, for your dreams, when checked against Source, are the thoughts of Source, the trajectory of Source expressing as you. In other words, a true dream, one that comes from Source, appears in your mind as thoughts, inclinations, and attractions to a certain activity, to a certain orientation. You define yourself by this dream and experience undergoing a journey to its realization.

Now, we are here to tell you, dear reader, that your journey to the realization of your dreams, including the dreams you did not choose, but which seemed to choose you, is still engaged. Your journey has not ended, the dreams are not unrealized; your story is not even remotely over. In fact, your journey continues full speed ahead to the fulfillment of your dreams. Perhaps the time frame does not meet with your approval, but your approval was never part of the scheme. This Life-Time experience you engage is like a train running on a track. You are still on the train. You are still running on the track. The train makes certain stops and has a certain ultimate destination, at which point it reverses direction and heads back to where it started from.

You have made stops on your journey. That does not mean you have reached your ultimate destination. So now you have it—your journey continues until the train reaches its ultimate destination. In this case, the ultimate destination is the greatest accomplishment of your Life-Time, an achievement which was determined by your greater self before you ever began the journey.

This achievement may not resemble your dreams in whole, or even in part, but you will recognize it when it happens as the sole reason you undertook the journey. If the journey contained no mystery, how boring for the traveler. Similarly, your peregrinations through the story, in pursuit of your dreams, all lead you to the ultimate destination. You are guaranteed to feel total satisfaction with your journey, as do all travelers in the Life-Time sequence. The destination must and is reached every single time. The real mystery is in knowing what the destination is.

Your dreams are the clues to your ultimate destination. They are the driving force of your train. But your dreams themselves are not the destination. It is always something far greater than a dream, far greater than you believe you can have. Again, dreams are the route to achievement of your destination. but they are not the destination, dear one. In this you have been sorely confused. Allow your dreams to announce themselves, allow them to drive your train and carry you to the prize. But let the prize appear in its own time, as it must, as it was pre-ordained before the journey began.

You may order and command your desires, dear one, even though your life is lived by Source. Or you may choose to allow yourself to be carried in the Source current. These two modes of being are both fully allowed in the story. Some alternate between the two, others choose one or the other. You may choose and then choose again. Your greater self embraces your choices, for it chooses through you. It manifests through you, it manifests in spite of you. To live consciously is to take up your responsibility of discerning the path of your true self, revealed from within by the daydreams, the urges, the thoughts and inclinations that come to you moment by moment.

A conscious player fully aligned with their greater self is aware of the direction the greater self wishes to go. They cannot wish for anything but what the greater self would have them be, do or have. This is the ultimate in non-resistance and a precursor to automatic transformation. They take no thought for the future because they know that the greater self designs the life of the story character. The story-you is not in charge; that is true. But when it surrenders fully to its leader, its own greater self, clarity of action arises.

So when you declare your commands in full recognition of oneness with your Source, you declare your surrender to your leader. In this melding with your greater self is forged the dreams of the greater you, dreams so much grander, so much richer than anything you ever imagined in your limited ideas of what life can offer you.

Do not hesitate to command and order your desires, dear one. For these are the wishes of your deepest, greatest self and the direct route to your ultimate destination. Concern yourself not with the meaning of your desires, nor should you compare the result with your ideal. Each command lifts you to the next stop on the train, no matter what the apparent outcome. Each reprocessed command lifts you even further.

You issue commands to consciously live the story as if you are the designer, knowing the greater you created the very design you command into being. It lives the design it created in the beginning, with every portion already known. Yet like the stationmaster on a train calling out the stops in a loud, clear voice, you declare into being each thread in the vast tapestry woven by your soul.

Source creates as much limitation as freedom so that we do not rise out of this dream of limitation in the physical illusion. Being the all and everything, Source enjoys itself by creating limited worlds of all kinds, worlds within worlds, none of it real, all just a play of consciousness, just an illusion of real, and so convincingly real, Source can lose itself in the story and explore being infinite selves in infinite varieties of existence.

Chapter 19

THE DREAM OF YOU

At night, dear reader, your dreams exist to give you a taste of creation as it is for your true self. Your true self has dreamed you and your world into existence in the same way you dream your night dreams and the world of your night dreams into existence. Your 'true' life is no more real or solid than your night life. Your story self and all of its relationships are no more real than the characters inhabiting your dreams, the world you inhabit no more real than the smoke and mirrors world of your dreams.

When you awaken from a night dream, the dream disintegrates instantly and all that is left is a memory, sometimes strong, often faint, of a place, a situation, an event. Sometimes the dream leaves a sense of healing or upliftment. Sometimes the dream frightens you such that you rejoice at being awake. Never is the dream more real than your daily life, yet its imprint sometimes pulls your attention to it over and over again, either to relive the pleasure or to resolve the pain.

Your dreams provide answers at times to questions of your daily life. Your dreams provide opportunities to explore different avenues you might take in your daily life. Yet your dreams are no more real than the mist on the bathroom mirror after your shower. The mist dispels the moment cool air enters the room. So does the mist of your night dreams dispel in the bracing light of day.

What is a dream, you ask? It is your memory of being Source, your reminder of the unreal nature of all creation, unreal in the sense that it is not physical, not solid as it appears, but simply an illusion of physicality and solidity.

Dear reader, remember what you have learned. You do not live a life. Life lives you. You do not create or construct your life story. You are created and constructed for the story. Your story is still underway. There is much to communicate at this time, most especially the truth about who you are in relation to the story.

You have correctly understood that you are born for the story of your life. There is no other story you can live and no other person you can be. This story is predetermined down to the last detail for the total creation of multiple intersecting stories in the illusion world. Each persona experiences the story as their own. Each is a spark of light unto their world. Dear reader, there is no such thing as a self made man. Personas love to claim responsibility for their seeming successes and deny responsibility for their seeming failures.

What follows is direct communication from Source, the one, true I.

In the real world of my creation no one is responsible for their successes and failures as I am the one and only Author of their story. Do characters in a book carry the responsibility for their lives, good, bad or indifferent? Or did the author infuse the character with characteristics suited to the life they lead, and did the author give the character their fate? You are a character in my book, dearest one, as are all personas.

I write your life story. Just like an author may know ahead exactly how the story plays out and works from an outline, I work from an outline, dear one. That outline is the original plan for your existence, start to finish. Yes, authors sometimes change their story and even discard the outline. But I know ahead exactly how I want to live the story of You.

In exploring all facets of my creation, I design characters for every possible type of story. To the character, my story may seem harsh and undeserving. Other characters feel richly rewarded beyond their value. Both ponder the meaning of these circumstances, but they only ponder their life's circumstances, such as they are, because they do not know or truly grasp that I am the creator of your world and I am the dreamer of your dream. My interests are not necessarily the interests of you, as my character. Therefore, the events of your life may not flow in a tidy manner or have reasonable results.

You see again and again that many of my characters do not allow themselves to dream and may lead what are termed 'small lives.' Many of my characters dream, but do not reach their dreams. Other of my characters don't even dream, but reach the heights anyway. And yet others dream and achieve their exact dream. You as my character are Me, All That Is, i.e., all the characters in expression at any one time.

When you identify with Me and not with your character, you are correctly focused and will not feel the sting of a difficult story. Knowing your true identity as the power and presence of God in human expression allows you to approach your story with curiosity and interest. What is the story calling from you? You see, dear one, my personas serve the story, not the other way around.

It is the ego of the unawakened character that believes themself to be all important. The unawakened character visualizes what he/she wants. If they get it, they assume they have the power to visualize what they desire and get it. If they don't get it, they may decide they didn't do it right and will try harder next time, or they may decide that visualizing doesn't work, when all along, I wrote the story, I wrote the visualizing scene, and I wrote the result. Do characters in a story act on the story and create their own destinies? Of course not; the author writes the destiny it chooses for that character.

You are asking, what about free will. Have I no free will? When you understand that the part of you labeled 'I' is an artifice and does not have any reality and that there is only one 'I', the All That Is expressing in infinite form, then you understand how it is that you have no free will. But the trade off is not so bad, is it? You trade off the little I with no free will for knowledge of the truth of your foundational identity as Me, the One Consciousness. If you do not take this step in your understanding, you remain deluded throughout your lifetime that you are an independent 'I' with a separate path and purpose.

Many of my characters retain this delusion throughout their life story and die believing they are a separate I. Why is this allowed, you ask? Because that is how I designed their story. But as soon as they abandon their body, they know instantly who they really are. And what a joyful discovery that is!

A life story in your illusion world is to Me like a brief dream at night is to you. The perception of time in the illusion enables every facet of your story to be fully experienced and explored in what is really just a fleeting moment of My Time. You are like a fantasy of my Mind, and I have infinite fantasies. Why am I so interested in creating characters and stories? This basic creative outflow is how I, Your true consciousness, express. It is not the only means of creation that I have, but it is a bulwark of my self-expression.

Awareness in the course of a story is pre-determined. A varying degree of awareness is allocated to each of my characters, ranging from virtually none to total Self-Realization. The scenes in your story where breakthroughs occur that appear to awaken you are designs of your story. Nothing happens that I do not author. Nothing happens that is not part of my plan.

For the many characters with an artificial 'I' and a belief in a reality separate and independent from Me, I am able to construct endlessly interesting scenarios of conflict, pain and loss, as well as progress, gain and victory, that quite fascinate Me. The awakened persona is of equal interest, but tends to create far less drama. An awakened persona is simply an 'I' who knows themself to be artificial and who orients themself to Me.

In the same way that the author of this book orients to Me for the writing of this book, an awakened persona orients to Me in the living of their story. Their story becomes a magical playground of possibility because they know that they exist to make the story happen. This approach imbues all moments of the story with presence of self and alertness to the signs and signals that most artificial 'I's usually ignore in the story.

The awakened ones intuit the meaning of signs and signals or they ask Me for guidance on their meaning. Either way, they cooperate with their story and are devoid of conflict no matter what the events of their story. Suffering in the story has only one cause. It is based on ignorance of the truth of existence. When you understand that I am living as you—that I am expressing in form as the story, I am sending events, signs and signals into your existence to ensure the story is carried forth as intended, I am creating all the details of your story including the problems and the solutions—when this is understood in a complete way, the end of suffering is at hand. For you realize that your life can only be what I make it and you have only one role, and that is to cooperate with the story.

In truth, you serve the story, rather than the other way around. The awakened one who understands they serve the story and deeply embraces this understanding at the core of their being finds Me there, smiling at them, their own true self, who was always there from the beginning, never far, never apart.

Some characters may feel unloved by Me when contemplating these words. After all, they reason, their story is difficult, painful, with exceptional burdens. Why have they been given this suffering when others are born to wealth and fortune?

All characters in my story are equally loved creations of My consciousness. They are literally extensions of My consciousness in the illusion world of their story. I am simply having virtual dreams, starring You. I am the You in these dreams, dear one. Try to understand, for those given the opportunity in their story to awaken, that we are one, there is only one Mind, one consciousness. Even if I express as numerous Higher Selves with numerous extensions of their own into stories of their own creation, it is all ultimately One Mind, One Consciousness, Me.

Direct communication from Source continues in the next chapter.

Chapter 20

WHO CREATES?

How then do you create reality, when Source, the one true I, creates every detail of your story? The answer is simple. You do not create reality. I create all that is, including your desire to create a certain reality and your desire to wrest power from the invisible and run with it.

The desire to manifest is the desire to be Me, which is a natural desire as you and I are one. But it is also the desire of someone who does not understand that you and I are already one in the story. If you did, it would be easy to comprehend that your purpose in the story is not to create reality.

Consider, dear one, how the deck is stacked upon your arrival on the scene, known as 'birth.' There is the experience of your birth, however that scenario occurred, the relatives and caretakers, the environment in which you are raised, the schools you attend and friends you acquire.

The birth experience brings with it the impetus for the next twenty-eight years of your life. There is no free will in the unfolding of these events, no unplanned relationships, jobs or experiences. Those who were part of your arrival team—the caretakers, relatives, family friends, etc.—remain throughout this phase, although your personal interaction with any given one may be limited or enhanced depending on the story. The person you marry, children you give birth to, the career you choose, or your lack of any of the above are all planned for the story.

If you think otherwise, dear one, ask yourself this about the illusion past—being who you were then, could you have done anything differently? An honest response is 'no,' though you may not understand why the answer can only be 'no.' It is 'no' because your story was preplanned from the beginning and carried out without hitch until the present moment.

Dear one, just as your true self, the great I of you, is Me, the All That Is, so too is the story you are living. In other words, that which you call your life is Me as well. I am both you and your Story! Can you not see that there is only one thing in action here—My consciousness. That is why there can only be a spiritual world; for My Consciousness is spiritual and everything that is is My Consciousness in expression. I do not create physical worlds, but only the illusion of physical worlds or any other kinds of worlds I can possibly conceive of. All creation is an illusion occurring within the field of My Consciousness, constructed with blocks of My Consciousness, and designed and enacted by My Consciousness.

You ask—how can it be? All the horror and devastation in the world is made by You? Here is the difficult truth, dear one. I am an Unconditioned Mind having dreams of every kind, exploring all manner of life, the entire range of expression and beyond into forms of expression you cannot imagine or conceive of in your current state. You are the character in my story for your life. That is all you need be concerned with. The other characters in your story have no more reality than you do—in other words, they are creations of my consciousness for your story. The story is all, dear one, and every element in your life serves the story. Do these elements as people have independent existence outside of your story? Ask yourself, do the characters in your night dreams have independent existence outside of your dream?

As Me, you are a great creator, capable of creating infinite characters, infinite stories, and infinite worlds. Is there some intermingling from one story to another? Sometimes I design stories to intermingle. Other times, your story is really a solitary dream with illusion characters that exist only for the story. I see your ears perk up.

You mean my wife and child are not real and only illusion characters for my story, you ask?

Are you not an illusion character in your story, dear one? They are illusion characters as well—creations of My consciousness, but in this case to serve your story, just as you are an illusion character created to serve your story. Remember, dear one, this is all a play of consciousness, an illusion story filled with illusion characters, including the lead character of your story, You. When you awaken fully, you understand that you have no independent existence, nor do any others in your story. Everything is a play of my consciousness and nothing can be outside my consciousness or my control.

When you understand that your story is a play of my consciousness, which is your consciousness when you are not focused in the story, you understand that I play within forms of limitation, within worlds of limitation, within minds of limitation. Why would I wish to do this? Because I want one thing—to express. Every creation is my expression and I revel in my expressions. All expression is joyous for me, even when, as a separate identity, you disconnect from my consciousness by labeling the story 'bad.'

I hear you crying out in indignation, do you mean that evil doings are joyous, are good?

Well, dear one, don't you enjoy a good thriller, a good crime drama in your movie theaters. Stories are the movie theater of my mind. The main character of each story is Me, appearing inside the story of my own creation so that I may have the full and complete experience of that story. In truth, creation cannot be otherwise—I can never be separate from my creation.

What about past lives you ask?

Dear one, in my infinite creation, infinite stories are run. I am the 'I' of each character in each story. Do you now understand there can be no such thing as a past life? Because I have an infinite consciousness and design each story individually, some stories have past life themes, but they are only to serve the story. In other words, when you watch a science fiction movie, do you automatically assume that the abilities of the characters, i.e., to travel back in time, to become another life form, are real? No. You understand that they are part of the story. In this way, I may design individual stories where characters have abilities or gifts such as contacting the dead or looking into the future or accessing past lives. These are stories, dear one, just like the science fiction movie, and do not imply factual truth.

Then what about personal growth and karma, I hear you ask? Don't we pay for our wrongdoings? Can't we grow and improve by our own choices and actions?

Let us take these questions one at a time.

Regarding personal growth, dear one, there is no such thing as personal growth as you are not a growing person! You are the consciousness of God, the All That Is, having a story experience. If the story shows you seem to mature, grow or change in some way, and that is viewed as positive in the story, that is the way that story was designed. I explore certain experiences in each story in the context of certain beliefs. By imbuing my characters with a certain belief system or world view, I create infinitely unique stories, as beliefs and mindsets can be infinitely varied.

As for karma, dear one, how can there be such a thing as karma, the 'what goes around comes around' theory? Nothing exists outside of My consciousness. I design each story and live it out. In some cases, the character experiences what may be termed payback or, on the other hand, a reward scenario, if it serves that story. In other cases, a character never receives their due, good or bad. Criminals may continue in their crime career until they die or stop. Other criminals are found out and imprisoned for the rest of their life. Either way, it is all just a story of my own creation.

The most difficult understanding for story characters is that of suffering. No character wants to suffer, and it seems as if suffering is imposed from the outside, often unbidden, often totally undeserved. The character feels as if they are being punished, for what they do not know. They may rail at the universe as to why these unhappy events have befallen them. Job, in the bible, is the classic example of this. All was taken from Job, his material wealth, his family, his health and his reputation, and he was left a destitute, desperate man. When he finally realizes that God is the author of his story and stops ranting against God, he accepts his fate and surrenders to God, which is the equivalent of surrendering to his story. In that moment, all is given back to him and he prospers and lives in joy for the rest of his long life.

The story of Job is instructive for all students of life. A story always brings a message for the character and it is the job(!) of the character to determine the meaning of the story. That determination is fueled by the signs and signals of your greater self, Me, the consciousness creating it all. You cannot get it wrong. If you set about to understand the meaning of an aspect of your story, you will receive the answer. The story is your guide on the path. Yes, the incidents and experiences, the moments of emptiness or doubt, all moments in your story are guides on your path. They have a reason for being, as nothing in the story is without a reason for being. And their reason is nothing less than to move you along the path of your story.

The story always successfully moves you along your path, either kicking and screaming or as a thoughtful detective following clues. The experience of the story is always about your reaction to the events. Conflict with the story creates a hell of your own making. I, your consciousness do not create your conflict. It is only your opposition to the truth—that you serve the story and are nothing less than a detective following clues in your own story—that peace is found. When you cooperate with the story, you save yourself, no matter what the outer scenario entails.

Now you know. I do not orchestrate your reaction to the story. The artificial 'I' is in almost constant resistance and reaction to the story, liking this, hating that, resisting this, embracing that. The life of an artificial 'I' who does not know who they are is predictable in certain parameters. It will be filled with enormous dissatisfaction, unhappiness and conflict with what-is. No matter, for their story chugs along unhindered by these emotional upheavals, as they are designed for that story and can do nothing but live it out as it was created in the beginning by My consciousness, the true self of all artificial 'I's.

The now moment brings with it the opportunity to 'stay with the story.' In that way, you orient towards Me, your own true consciousness. The proper orientation to me in the story is one of cooperation and questions. You ask the questions and I give the answers. You look for the answers in the signs and signals of the moment. By calmly seeking My guidance on your life path, you understand the meaning of all difficult aspects of your story and can find the positive purpose behind it all.

Yes, dear one, there is good news! All stories have a positive purpose. All events within each person's story have an ultimately positive purpose for that person. The positive purpose may not be discernible for some time during the story, but each event sooner or later reveals its true meaning and higher purpose for the story. The job of the story character is to cooperate with the story and be a detective in following the clues I send.

I, your true self, am Invisible during your virtual story and can only communicate indirectly—through signs and signals, through words as I am doing here, and through specific occurrences or chance meetings, those events that just seem to happen to you. As your armless, legless, voiceless guide in the story, I transform each story into a treasure hunt. When approaching your story in this way, the fun and joy of being a character in your story, lived out within My consciousness, is magnified.

Again, I may remind you, the same story can be lived in a state of resistance, generating misery and depression, or in a state of cooperation, generating joy and happiness. It all depends on your attitude. Do I reward good attitudes? No! And No again! The story carries on no matter what your attitude. But the subjective experience of the story as joyful and fun is its own reward.

There is a belief that if you cooperate with the story, the story itself transforms or improves. Dear one, the story experience is not a test of your cooperative abilities. It is simply a dream focusing on certain facets of experience I wish to explore from the point of view of a specific persona.

Have I created a law which transforms a non-resistant attitude into an improved story experience? In other words, will you have more success, more wealth, more love, more material things because you are non-resistant? No, not necessarily. There is no correlation between a non-resistant attitude and a better story. The story cannot be improved upon. It is preset from the beginning, just as an author outlines the story for the characters in her novel. The author wishes to explore the story from the perspective of these characters, and may also wish to comment on the story or the characters as she goes along.

Your story exists as an idea in My Mind. Your response to the story tells another story, the subcreation, in other words a secondary version of the story of my creation. Your story is told through the emotions and reactions triggered by the events of your story. My story is embodied in the people and events of your story, which are all geared for an ultimately positive purpose. When your story becomes one with my story and we are not at cross purposes, a beautiful harmony is created and your story becomes a happy tale.

Dear one, all stories are happy tales IF the persona understands who he or she is, i.e., God in expression, what their story is, i.e., a dream in the mind of God, and aligns with the story to live it in a cooperative manner.

What if horrible things befall a persona in a story?

The sting from all so-called horrible events in a story is part of the persona's subcreation. It is an emotional response or reaction to the event based on the persona's belief system. The belief system has been honed by years of associating certain feelings or energy states with certain occurrences until they are automatic. This automated aspect of the persona manifests as a negative response to an event, or conversely, a positive response to an event.

When a persona knows who they really are—God in expression—and understands that they are simply engaged in a temporary dream experience within their own greater consciousness, there should be no fear or concern about anything that happens. Now you understand that it is the belief about the way things should happen and the attachment to life going a certain way that causes the considerable pain many players feel.

An awakened player does not take their life story any more seriously than they would a board game. The game begins and ends. It contains certain events and results. These events and results are whatever they are and the game is over. Yes, there may be a certain intensity in the playing of the game, a certain exhilaration in playing a rousing game, a certain melancholy in playing a losing game, but these emotions are passing, are recognized as automated responses to the game triggered by the player's belief system.

The awakened player knows that they don't know the real meaning of anything that happens. A happy event could presage a disturbing experience. An unhappy event could precede an amazing breakthrough. The key point here is that the dream of your virtual life is in constant flux, it is fluid, ephemeral, and its meaning can transform in an instant. The challenge is to remain open in every moment to the next moment and the next moment, and the next, without needing to clamp down on an interpretation of that moment or lock in the feelings that arise as something permanent. A light touch in one's life is the right touch.

Imagine for a moment that your physical body is a spacesuit, an encasement within which you operate on this planet, much the way an astronaut operates in space. The astronaut peers out of the viewing apparatus in his suit and sees the environment, sees the other astronauts lumbering around in their suits. The suit enables the astronaut to breathe and protects them from the elements. It is an indispensable part of their visit to another planet, without which their mission could not be accomplished.

Your physical body is a virtual sensory apparatus that enables you to negotiate your virtual world in the exact same way as an astronaut negotiates a planetary world. It gives you an identifiable presence along with the continuity of story that it implies.

You are suited up for your journey, so to speak, the moment you are born. As you launch into a virtual world, in this case, what is called planet Earth, your passage is assured. The moment you arrive you board the train of your destiny and ride it in, inexorably, to your final destination. After the story, you marvel at the rip-roaring time you had, no matter whether it felt happy or sad when you were there. It is always a rip-roaring tale and a wondrous one at that, something that you will ponder and relive in consciousness, savor if you will, until you have extracted all the gold from the ore. That is why it is a happy tale. You always return with gold after you reach your final destination on your journey.

Chapter 21

THE QUANTA OF BEING

God is All That Is, dear reader. God is not only the story, but God is also 'you,' the experiencer of the story, and the substance of all that exists beyond the story. From this perspective let us take a look at your thorny problem whatever it may be; virtual troubles one might accurately say. Yes, it is a virtual reality and the trouble is only virtual. It is not real, permanent, lasting or solid, like everything else in a virtual world.

So what do you do when presented with the illusion of trouble? Laugh, dear one, laugh heartily as it is a true comedy. Many personas might call your situation tragic, but it is genuine comedy. Why? Because in your true identity you are the creator of everything. You lack nothing and have everything. You have all power in your true identity. Nothing can control you, harm you, or limit you in your true identity. That is why the only response to troubles in a virtual world is a hearty laugh.

Now that you have laughed at your condition, you are ready to send out your radar to discern what is the next stop on your journey, meaning, what is the action you are being asked to take, if any, in the face of your circumstances.

To discern the direction of your train, you may tune in to your infinite self. Remember, dear reader, it is you, the player, who serves the story and not the story that serves the player. Ask yourself, the higher part of self, what must I do to serve the story at this juncture? When asking such a question, you must be prepared for the unexpected, you must be prepared to open choicelessly to the unknown.

From that expansive space, allow the answer to take form. It may come as a vision or as words you hear in your mind. It may come as something you read or someone who enters your life, as something you notice in the environment or something that is said to you.

Know this—you cannot ask that question in a spirit of openness and inquiry without getting your answer. You will always receive the true and correct answer when you approach your greater self with an attitude of service and a consciousness of choiceless awareness.

Take a moment to recall the thorny problem besetting you. Now ask yourself, what is the story asking of me? How can I serve the story as it relates to this thorny problem? Empty your mind of all the likely and expected responses and allow yourself to enter an infinite space where anything is possible. Say to yourself, I am now creating the space for the true and correct answer. The true and correct answer, coming from my infinite self, now makes its appearance in my life.

Ask, can I know the correct answer about my troubles now? If the answer is yes, then attune carefully for the answer and write it down. If the answer is no, you can be certain that the answer will be obvious at a later time. Finally, ask if there is anything at all you need to know at this point in time, and note the response.

By engaging in this form of inquiry, you establish a stronger connection to your greater self, the creator of your story, and foster the correct attitude towards your life and the events thereof.

When dreams don't come true it signifies that taking a certain direction was necessary for your story. However, actually arriving where you thought you were heading was not part of the story and was not necessary for your story. This may be a truly hard pill to swallow, as many broken hearts litter the sides of the roads of those on the journey through their stories. But if a poll were taken, it is actually more common to not realize your biggest dream than it is to realize it. And for those who do realize their dream they can look forward to encountering its downside, making it not quite the dream they had imagined.

There is a certain balance that is maintained in each story, a balance of pain and pleasure, of success and failure, of love and hate, of joy and sadness. This balance is built into the program for each virtual story. Therefore, you can be certain that the player who seems to lead a charmed life will experience its opposite before their story completes. The downtrodden individual will have their day in the sun, and so on. These pendulum swings are relative, meaning they are designed to be significant for that persona in that story and may not be observed by or significant for any other characters in that story.

The life experience is a pendulum, swinging back and forth from one side to the other. Most stories are woven with a strong mixture of good and bad so that the player can have a wide range of experience simultaneously. In other words, the weave is like musical counterpoint, one line plays against another, and yet another, and yet another, each having their own distinct flavor, each having their own pendulum pattern, while together equaling a whole.

In a virtual story the counterpoint reflects the themes being explored simultaneously throughout all levels of that story. The themes create a prism of events and emotions, representing both the linear or surface level of the story, i.e., 'the story that is told,' and the other levels of the story, which include the emotional, the spiritual and the multidimensional.

Chapter 22

Undoing the Chains of Judgment

Every story is a rich tapestry far beyond the obvious. There are no wasted lives or wasted stories. In the emotional level of everyday life the subcreation is told. By that I mean the second story; what events meant to that persona, what experiences triggered emotional change, what degree of awakening to truth occurred. The richest part of the story is lived through the second story. Yet it is also the part of the story that is less in touch with reality than any other.

In the first story, you have the outer events and experiences of your train ride. This part of the story plays out from a customized blueprint created by your greater self. These are the experiences you cannot avoid, the cornerstone events and acts of the story, beginning with your birth, its setting, locale and constituents, and ending with your death, its setting, locale and constituents.

The second story is the emotions experienced in each moment of the journey through the story. As mentioned earlier, the more you understand the nature of reality, the more you understand that emotions are completely arbitrary and that strong emotional reactions to the events of life, good or bad, are signs of strong attachment to the story and belief in its reality.

The more one embraces the truth of one's immortal infinite self and the temporary nature of the virtual story, the emotional impact of events is lessened and there is a more playful and fearless relationship to the story.

In the second story, the truth of your relationship to the story is revealed moment by moment. When the story grips your soul in such a way as to trigger strong emotions, you are lost in the story. When the story leaps out to grab you and you resist its pull, maintaining a modicum of balance, you are conscious in the story.

A battle takes place every day in the lives of every character in a story. What belief will dominate? The awakened player recognizes the battle for their mind, not to mention their soul, which is waged in the story through the emotional or second story. The awakened player jumps aside like a ninja master and avoids the sword thousands of times per day. This dodging of bullets becomes a way of life for the awakened player who understands that the true story is lived in the second story and, therefore, strives to maintain an awareness of their true condition as infinite consciousness on a temporary journey.

The third story, or the spiritual level, is your communion with your greater self whilst in the story and your attunement to the signs and signals from your greater self. The third story is signified by cooperation with the story and an attitude of service to the story, knowing that God is the story inasmuch as God, the Infinite Self, is the All and the Everything.

The fourth story, or multidimensional level, is not accessible from the story. It is mentioned here only to provide a complete picture of what a story really is in its totality. All levels of a story unfold throughout other dimensions or virtual worlds of consciousness where the Infinite Self resides and expresses ad infinitum. Although the multidimensional aspect of the story cannot be accessed while within the story, it is available upon exit and yields the true meaning of the story and its true value and purpose.

Given this expanded introduction to what a Life-Time really is, let us take another look at what happens in the story. The point of this chapter is to explain how it is that you, the player, are not responsible for the events in your story. You have a range of choice regarding the emotions, and you have the option of becoming aware at the spiritual level. However, even these degrees of freedom are customized for each story, and in many cases are quite limited. In other words, the range of choice regarding emotional response and spiritual awareness is customized according to the needs of the specific story.

If you have read this far into this book, then you can rest assured that you are a player whose story has been customized for the widest possible freedom of emotional and spiritual experience. The wider the degrees of freedom, the more truth can be accessed, understood and applied.

Now I can hear you ask, do you mean that people who perform evil deeds are not responsible for their actions?

It is difficult to accept the truth that good and evil are constructs of virtual stories and have no lasting impact beyond the story. Everyone gets up at the end of the day and is infinite, just like the actor who died in a movie gets up off the ground, dusts himself off and goes home for dinner.

The virtual world encompasses every conceivable variation of experience. All is permitted within the totality of stories being run. All is *not* permitted within the specific story you are running in that a blueprint is designed with the specifics for your story.

Most stories do not engage with the world of extreme good or extreme evil. But some stories play out in the extremes. For those players an enormous amount of spiritual support is given to assist them through those journeys no matter which side they are on. Even within the extremes, there are pendulum swings, there are second and third stories and there is a multidimensional level wherein lies the higher meaning and purpose of it all.

But let us focus on your story, everyman's story so to speak of their search for the good life. This story is characterized by the pursuit of total well-being: abundance, success, love and health. Let us call it the four-square story, which is a dominant modality among virtual journeys. Inevitably the story goes awry. You are acclimated to many small deviations from the four-square dream, but when larger deviations than expected occur, a problem is perceived. The story may be beset with numerous problems in all segments of the four-square. Sometimes it only takes one critical problem in one part of the square to throw the whole story off-kilter.

A persona tends to judge themself and others by the way in which their life seems to align with a successful four-square story. We say 'seems to align' because stories cannot be known by looking in, as if through a window. The true story is only known by the persona living it.

A rush to judgment arises automatically in response to the illusion of a problem in one or more quadrants of the story. The first to be judged is the persona, who judges themself, as all players know on some level that they have designed the story. Frustration quickly follows as does anger over the turn of events in the story.

More specifically, the player realizes that a wrench has been thrown into the works by their greater self, but for what reason? The player can't really understand the value of problems or difficulties whatsoever and would feel more supported if things went their way. Thus, an internal tantrum takes place as an expression of intense resistance to the unwanted development. As a result, the second to be judged is the greater self that designed the story from a place of infinite consciousness.

Now you have a story character who is furious and disappointed with themself and with their greater self or God. The judgment domino effect does not end there, however. It then moves on to all others involved with the problem or in any way associated with it, even if only in the mind of the character. The story character condemns those who contributed to their problem and eventually works out in their mind a list of every guilty player whose presence, actions or input set the stage and/or directly contributed to the current problem.

Given this judgment domino effect, we may assume that characters in the virtual story come wrapped in chains of judgment. One character wrapped in chains interacts with another character wrapped in chains and these chains only add to the difficulty of relating to one other. Therefore, two characters do not really interact. Two characters plus their chains of judgment interact, with uncertain and disappointing results.

How are characters released from these chains of judgment? There is only one way. The player must remember the truth of their condition. By reminding yourself that you are on a temporary journey within a virtual reality, you begin the process of connecting with truth.

By then reminding yourself that you yourself in your Infinite consciousness designed the journey you are embarked upon, as well as the very event that is so distasteful, you further connect with truth.

By then allowing the story to simply be what it is without any need to alter it, you demonstrate emotional acceptance of your true condition even if you are not able to fully feel that acceptance.

At that point, you have created the fertile soil for a new idea, a new course of action, or some solution to your situation. By testing carefully for the emotional resonance of this new idea or solution, you can then determine which action the story asks you to take.

Imagining the correct action will bring a sense of completeness long before results are seen. When an imagined action or series of actions bring a sense of completeness, this is the correct path in the story even though the problem may still seem to be present.

Concluding Thoughts

As a servant of the story, your life is immensely simplified. By doing your best to give the story what it appears to be asking of you, you move in peace through the journey that is your life. By giving up the egoistic position in your story, along with its demand that the story meet your requirements, you take the correct relationship to your life. The chains of judgment are undone and this automatically allows a higher vibrational story to unfold, one which contains the potential for a richer and more fulfilling experience.

The perspective you have of who and what you are, what your life is, and who and what everyone else is, determines the emotional tone of your journey. Your perspective impacts every detail of your daily experience to form the second story, otherwise known as the subcreation. The subcreation is the real story as far as the story-you is concerned. It is how you feel in the moment by moment living out of the story. But the subcreation is subjective and is the part of your journey that can be completely altered by you. The fastest way to alter the subcreation is to change your perspective. The perspective most closely aligned with truth offers the most joy in the moment. That option always exists for you, but you must claim it in order to activate it.

The perspective that guarantees joy, which is the true nature of infinite consciousness and which can never be denied you, comes from taking the non-egoic position in relation to your story. You exist to serve the story. The story has been written by your Infinite Self. It is a temporary journey. It has a multi-dimensional purpose that transcends any meaning that you may attribute to it, but which you can never know while in the story.

The emotional disturbance caused by a subjective loss of meaning while in the story is symbolic of recognizing the greater truth that meaning cannot be known while in the story. You serve the story on trust, blind faith, understanding that you survive the story, that you will be restored to your infinite consciousness, and that you will reap the full rewards of your journey.

You adopt the perspective that everyone else exists to serve their story and are designed for their story as you are for yours. Therefore, you understand that people do not succeed against the odds or pull themselves up by the bootstraps. They do not possess ineffable genius or talent that is denied you. They are not luckier than you even if their story seems brighter.

Because each character is designed for their story they cannot be anything but what the story requires. For this reason, there is no call to feel superior or inferior to anyone. Other personas are living out their stories, the ones invented by infinite consciousness, and they are no more or less than you; a temporary persona in a virtual story pre-designed by infinite consciousness, possessing all the necessary qualities, talents, nuances and quirks required for that story.

People do not rise up out of the mud, so to speak, to become iconic figures by their own Herculean efforts, although it may appear that way. No character is deserving of worship, as the persona does not create itself from the locus of the persona.

Infinite consciousness creates the appropriate persona to serve a particular story conceived by infinite consciousness. The persona cannot deviate from the story it serves, and the story cannot deviate from the consciousness that created it.

Before you go, please make sure to download your bonus report, "How to Deconstruct a Troublesome

Situation." It will help you maintain a peaceful inner state by showing you how to clear and detach from the negative thoughts and emotional reactions that threaten to upset your day. To get your bonus gift, just go to http://bit.ly/DeconstructSituation.

DID YOU ENJOY THIS BOOK?

Dear Reader,

Thank you for reading this book. If you enjoyed ***Matrix Man: How To Become Enlightened, Happy &Free In An Illusion World,*** I'd really appreciate it if you would take a moment to go online to leave a review on Amazon. Your review matters because it will help me to reach more readers who will discover this book thanks to your review.

Thanks again, and wishing you the very best,

S. F. Howe

BOOKS BY S. F. HOWE

MIND · BODY · SPIRIT

HIGHER CONSCIOUSNESS

Matrix Man: How To Become Enlightened, Happy & Free In An Illusion World

The author reveals a new reality paradigm that will liberate you from the limiting beliefs and programs that prevent a joyful and fulfilling life. Available in print and digital editions.

The Top Ten Myths Of Enlightenment: Exposing The Truth About Spiritual Enlightenment That Will Set You Free!

Essential reading for spiritual seekers. What no one else will tell you to help you avoid the pitfalls of the spiritual journey. Available in print and digital editions.

The Bringer: Waking Up To The Mind Control Programs Of The Matrix Reality

For those seeking freedom from cultural indoctrination, this book offers a higher dimensional perspective on the most ingrained and unquestioned aspects of everyday life. Available now in the digital edition and soon available in print.

PLANT INTELLIGENCE

Secrets Of The Plant Whisperer: How To Care For, Connect, And Communicate With Your House Plants

A plant whisperer reveals the hidden truth about plants and why relating to them in a conscious way is vital for their health and well-being. Available in print and digital editions.

Your Plant Speaks!: How To Use Your Houseplant As A Therapist

Let your house plant solve your problems! Discover the little known art of receiving life coaching from your favorite indoor plant.
Coming Soon!

PERSONAL GROWTH

Vision Board Success: How To Get Everything You Want With Vision Boards!

A powerful technique for achieving your goals and manifesting your desires. Available in print and digital editions.

Sex Yoga: The 7 Easy Steps To A Mind-Blowing Kundalini Awakening!

A technique for activating the chakras to induce a powerful kundalini experience. Available in print and digital editions.

Morning Routine For Night Owls: How To Supercharge Your Day With A Gentle Yet Powerful Morning Routine!

Morning rituals aren't only for morning people, and they don't have to be rough and tumble or performed at top speed to set up a perfect day. Welcome to the world of the gentle yet powerful wake-up routine for night owls! Available in print and digital editions.

CONSCIOUS HEALTH

Transgender America: Spirit, Identity, And The Emergence Of The Third Gender

A higher consciousness perspective on the Transgender Agenda; what it is and why it is being rolled out at breakneck speed to socially engineer a gender dysphoria epidemic. Available in print and digital editions.

When Nothing Else Works: How To Cure Your Lower Back Pain Fast!

The simple method that no doctor will ever tell you about. Requires no drugs, no surgery, and no special equipment. Available in print and digital editions.

ABOUT THE AUTHOR

S. F. Howe is a transformational psychologist, author and spiritual teacher. Howe began teaching psychology at the university level while a doctoral candidate in clinical psychology, and went on to work in hospitals and clinics for more than 25 years as a psychotherapist, staff psychologist, clinical program consultant and director of chemical dependency and psychiatric programs.

In the midst of graduate studies, a profound spiritual awakening led to a complete reevaluation of the author's life path. Thus began a spiritual journey along the road less traveled, extending far beyond clinical psychology, conventional reality paradigms and both traditional religion and new age spirituality.

While engaged in a unique, ongoing process of discovery, the author enjoys sharing with others an ever-expanding understanding of the true nature of reality. This has resulted in Howe's noted books and teachings on the subjects of higher consciousness, conscious health, personal growth and plant intelligence.

Howe's primary intention is to bring peace and an end to mental suffering by guiding others on a well-worn path to truth and expanded awareness. Many of those who have experienced Howe's input and presence report emotional and physical healing, life-changing realizations and dramatic personal transformation.

S. F. Howe may be contacted for speaking and teaching engagements. Please direct all inquiries to info@diamondstarpress.com.

FREE GIFT

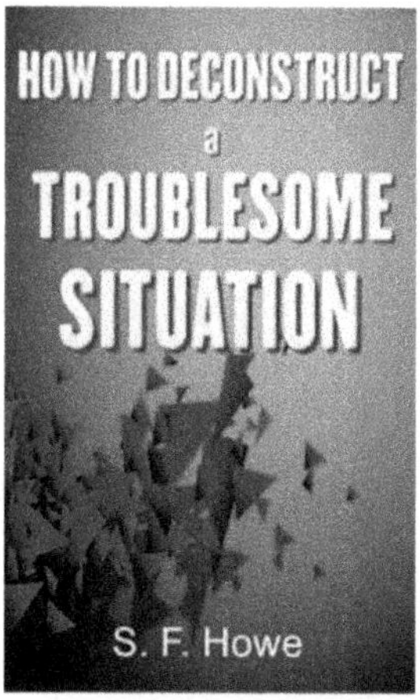

As my thanks to you for reading ***Matrix Man: How To Become Enlightened, Happy & Free In An Illusion World,*** I would like you to have the free bonus report, "How to Deconstruct a Troublesome Situation." This bonus gift is an important addition to the material in this book and will help you implement its teachings.

If you apply the technique in this report, you will not only discover the many ways in which your mental and emotional conditioning interferes with your peaceful inner state but you will also learn how to clear and detach from the negative emotional reactions that upset your day. To get your free gift, just go to http://bit.ly/DeconstructSituation.

www.ingramcontent.com/pod-product-compliance
Lightning Source LLC
Chambersburg PA
CBHW071424090426
42737CB00011B/1566
* 9 7 8 0 9 7 7 4 3 3 5 5 1 *